Austin Stouffer brilliantly captures the heart of the Bible's passion for releasing women fully into ministry. Drawing on powerful appeals to the redemptive mindset of the Scriptures, Dr. Stouffer breaks through the encrusted layers of tortured and stale interpretations that have been used to deprive the church of the rich ministry gifts that the Spirit of Jesus has placed within women. *95 More for the Door* deserves to be posted prominently on every "castle door" of the evangelical kingdom!

~Dr. Guy S. Saffold, Executive Director of Ministries
Power to Change Ministries (formerly called Campus Crusade, Canada)

95 More for the Door is an interesting, provocative book that is easy reading for lay people but deals in depth with most of the questions raised regarding "women's roles" in the church, home and society. People who are honestly interested in what the Bible says on this topic will find this book very helpful. Austin Stouffer, a pastor and marriage and family therapist, brings his vast knowledge of the Bible and human nature to deal sympathetically with the questions and traditions many Christians struggle with concerning this subject. The take-off on C. S, Lewis' *Screwtape Letters"* in the Appendix, titled, "The Rev. Mrs.—Satan's Greatest Fear" is alone worth the price of the book.

~Alvera Mickelsen, Author and former teacher
Bethel University and Wheaton College

Stouffer walks the reader through the minefield of whether or not there is biblical evidence for equity in the role of women in public ministry. If your viewpoint is that there isn't, to secure your position you will want to face his list and argue why he is wrong. If, however, you are neutral with respect to this question, his material will help you see various ideas and texts that serve to outline the debate. If you agree with Stouffer, his thesis will assist you in constructing a framework for discussion. Regardless of your view, this study is most helpful in wrestling with a ministry and calling issue that can't be avoided as we live out our calling to make Christ known to our world.

~Dr. Brian C. Stiller, President
Tyndale University College and Seminary, Toronto, ON

Whether or not you agree with every thesis point here, think through the implications of this whole study: so much of Scripture does challenge us to rethink our gender prejudices. Thanks, Austin, for helping us see that.

~Rev. Don Gillett, Pastor
Grace Evangelical Free Church, Thunder Bay, ON

Austin Stouffer brings the light of Scripture to bear upon one of the greatest handicaps facing the church—gender prejudice. By doing so, Stouffer stands as part of the reformist tradition in providing significant biblical, moral and logical clarity to the modern concerns of gender, authority and the Church. The book is helpful to popular and academic audiences.

~Dr. Mimi Haddad, President
Christians for Biblical Equality, Minneapolis, MN

95
MORE
for the
DOOR

a ~~layman's~~ layperson's biblical guide to today's
GENDER REFORMATION

Austin H. Stouffer

95 MORE FOR THE DOOR
A Layperson's Biblical Guide to the Gender Reformation

By Austin H. Stouffer

Cover photo: Ron Jason, Ron Jason Photography

WORD ALIVE PRESS

Printed by Word Alive Press
131 Cordite Road, Winnipeg, MB R3W 1S1
www.wordalivepress.ca

to

eleanor
kirsten
heidi

my wife
my daughters
my equals

always

INTRODUCTION

This book will make more sense if you read this introduction first. It is my hope that you'll see that, although my message is for everyone, I especially want men to read it. At the same time, I have a hunch a lot of women will read it first and say, "Oh, I want a copy of this for my husband (father, pastor, boss, etc.)." If you can imagine yourself or someone close to you saying one or more of the following statements, this book is meant for you (and them).

1. "I've always thought that men and women aren't quite equal. I don't know why, but in a marriage, it just makes sense that the man is boss."

2. "I think it works best when the husband is 'head of the house,' as long as he does that in a very loving way."

3. "In our marriage, my husband is always the boss and makes *all* the decisions. Sometimes I feel more like a slave than a wife, but I guess that's God's plan."

4. "My husband sometimes reminds me that God has placed him as a 'priest' over our house and given him the awesome responsibility of making the final decisions."

5. "In our church, there are certain ministries that women just cannot do, like sit on a Board of Elders or preach a sermon."

6. "I'm OK with women preaching now and then, as long as we don't ordain them to be official pulpit pastors."

7. "As a pastor, I'd love to let women be ordained, but I'm deeply committed to the inspiration of Scripture, and my Bible strictly says that the role of Pastor or Elder is reserved for *men*!"

Can you hear yourself saying statements like these? I sure can—or at least, I sure used to! It might help you to know two things about me.

First, I've recently retired from full-time ministry in a well-known evangelical denomination which, at the time of writing this, does not ordain women. Many of our churches use women in various areas of ministry, but many do not. Women can be "credentialed" for some ministries (Chaplaincy, Christian Education, etc.) but only men can be ordained to pulpit/pastoral positions, and only then are they called "Reverend." Women can attend our seminaries, even teach in them, but only male teachers can be ordained.

Secondly, during these years I have also been a marriage counselor and continue to maintain my clinical membership in the American Association for Marriage and Family Therapy. I have counseled thousands of couples and have become increasingly saddened, hearing stories of women who have lived with domineering, sometimes abusive husbands. Many of these couples did not attend church or have any specific religious beliefs, but many did. Some deeply committed Christian women have related incidents about Bible-believing fathers or husbands who insisted it was their God-given duty to make all decisions for their families, often in very inappropriate ways. "Rationalized" stories of child abuse—even sexual abuse and incest—were not infrequent in sessions with seemingly deeply committed Christian couples.

The secular world would place me solidly in the "conservative" theological camp, and I accept that. Yet, I fail to understand how so many sincere, fervent, Bible-believing Christians throughout history have continued to insist on only one possible interpretation of Scripture passages relating to women's roles, when those same passages have legitimately been interpreted to mean the very opposite *by equally educated and dedicated conservative scholars*! Over the past few decades, many excellent books have been written to explain that the Bible really does treat men and women as equal in Christ, church and community. Check out the References at the back of this book; you'll find many conservative authors who take the "inspiration and authority" of the Bible very seriously, yet take gender equality just as seriously. Many of these books are written mainly to pastors, church administrators and highly educated people in general. We need these books, because they offer academic validity to the movement. But I think there's a market for explaining this very important topic in ordinary street language. I think it's time we stopped teaching lies about male "headship" and female "submission" and let the Bible say what it intended to say two thousand years ago. In Heaven, or here on earth, there can be no second category of God's children.

So, what's the bottom line? Maybe we need another "Reformation." After all, it's been five centuries since the Protestant Reformation shook things up. This new reformation targets both Protestants and Catholics—not to mention every other diverse religious group and political party out there. It's time for the whole world to embrace a *Gender Reformation*.

Most people have heard of Dr. Martin Luther, leader of the Protestant Reformation in the 1500s. Don't confuse him with Dr. Martin Luther King, the great US civil rights leader assassinated in the 1960s, although both men dramatically changed our world. This earlier Luther, a promising young German theologian and Augustinian monk, became furious with the Church's brazen fundraising scheme to build St. Peter's Cathedral. Here's how it worked: for a large enough donation to the building fund, donors were given a "Certificate of Indulgence," a piece of paper stating that the punishment for their sin(s) had been removed and their (and their relatives') stay in Purgatory would be shortened in proportion to the size of their donation to the building fund. The movement even had its own theme song or jingle which, loosely translated, advised the followers, "As soon as the coin in the coffer rings / The soul from Purgatory springs" (Bainton, 60). Catholics see Purgatory as a place where they end up after death for a time of purification by suffering before entering Paradise. No wonder many saw this certificate as a license to keep "indulging" in their pet sins.

Intending only to inform and correct the church he so deeply loved, Luther took pen and paper and prayerfully, methodically constructed his now world-famous "Ninety-Five Theses." Simply put, he organized his grave concerns about what he called "The Power and Efficacy of Indulgences," as practiced by the church of his day, into ninety five short statements or "theses" for discussion. Then he allegedly tacked this document on the chapel door at the University of Wittenberg for all students and professors to consider. The date: October 31, 1517—All-Hallows Eve, or Halloween. Soon, all of Germany was talking, and the young seminary professor, who only wanted debate, became a household name throughout Europe and England. If it happened today, all major television networks would cover it. Talk-show hosts would preempt all other guests and get Luther on the show. Edith Simon, in her book, *Luther Alive,* described it well: "Unexpectedly, mysteriously, somehow it had struck a universal chord which set the whole keyboard of Christianity humming" (138).

What does all this have to do with gender equality? Only one thing: *Reformation.* Not that I expect this book to set the whole keyboard of Christianity humming (although I wouldn't mind if it did), and I certainly don't want to split God's worldwide family. Rather, I want us all to simply, prayerfully, honestly consider "reforming" our views of how we see men and women in church, home and workplace.

I wonder why Martin Luther decided to write exactly ninety-five thesis statements. Why not fifty, or one hundred? Even though a definite structure is evident as you read them, there's a lot of overlap in the points he raises. I began wondering how many places there are in the Bible that relate to men and women being equal. It didn't take long to find thirty, then forty. Six months later, I had over ninety! With a bit of organizing, I settled on Luther's number.

What you now have in your hand is my "ninety-five theses" on gender equality. Each chapter, or thesis, begins with a short, bold-type statement, about the same length as Luther's thesis statements, followed by a few lines or paragraphs of explanation. The theses are chronological, beginning with pertinent verses from the first book of the Old Testament (Genesis) all the way through to the last book in the New Testament (Revelation), although I don't use every book in between. Where the same point is made in different places, I usually deal with the topics as they come up chronologically, then cross-reference them. Whether you agree or disagree with my structure or the number of points I chose, it doesn't really matter. What matters is that you realize that there are many places in the Bible where you *can* (and many think should) conclude that God intended men and women to be equally affirmed and gifted, whether to lead in society, to parent in the home or to minister in church.

By now you will have noticed that I want this book to sound the way most people talk to each other at work, in the kitchen or on the golf course. Actually, that was Martin Luther's idea as well: to help ordinary people discuss, question, understand, interpret and practice what the Bible really means without any superimposed agenda from the experts. Here and there I'll get a bit technical on sticky passages, but in general, this book is meant to be an easy read for everyone. Then, if you want to compare my thoughts with some heavy duty answers from the experts, order a few books from the References at the back.

This book is not meant to be an encyclopedia of gender equality in various cultures throughout history, and I'm not trying to explain it as a sociologist, anthropologist or psychologist would. There are many informative books out there that do all that. *My only reason for writing this book is to show you that there are at least 95 places in the Old and New Testaments that either assume, teach directly or can reasonably be explained to teach that women and men were meant to be treated, gifted, appointed or ordained in exactly the same way, whether by God, Jesus, the early church, the writers of the Bible, centuries of history, contemporary society—or even conservative Christians.*

I want to thank some significant authors and leaders in this area who have assisted me greatly through their writings and/or personal comments. The spark was first fanned into flame as I bounced my doctoral thesis topic off Roberta Hestenes and Lou Smedes at Fuller Theological Seminary three decades ago. That flame was further ignited as I devoured the scholarly writings of some of the giants in the field: Gretchen Gabelein Hull, Richard and Catherine Clark Kroeger, Alvera Mickelsen (my endorser, wise mentor and patient advisor), Mary Stewart Van Leeuwen, Gilbert Bilezikian, Craig Keener, Rebecca Merrill Groothuis and many, many others who have built up an impressive, credible academic foundation. Their writings and personal advice have been deeply appreciated. They, together with the outstanding ongoing work of the staff at Christians for Biblical Equality (www.cbeinternational.org) are slowly, steadily turning the tide that has minimized, muffled and misused half of God's church for over two thousand years.

Final thanks goes to Larissa Bartos (and staff) at Word Alive Press, Winnipeg, Canada. More than once her gentle suggestions magically morphed my stumbling sentences into what I had intended to say.

Just as I was sending this book to press, I received a chat-line e-mail from one of my endorsers, a long-time friend and colleague dating back to our Trinity Western Seminary days: Dr. Guy Saffold, now with Power to Change Ministries (formerly Campus Crusade, Canada). He has convincingly captured the major intent of my book as well as the ongoing tensions the topic will continue to raise. He writes:

> "There are different convictions about what totally truthful, fully accurate and utterly scrupulous interpretation and application of Scripture according to its Spirit-intended purpose requires. Some look at Scripture with the most honest and spiritually sensitive eyes they can muster under the prayerful direction of the Holy Spirit and conclude that the Bible, when the text is interpreted with total faithfulness using every valid and sound principle of

hermeneutics, simply, plainly and truthfully does not teach that women should or must function under male authority. Others conclude that it does. It is a thorny difference among people who take every word of Scripture as the absolutely truthful revelation of the mind of God."

~Austin H. Stouffer

THESIS SUMMARIES

APPENDIX I

APPENDIX II

THESIS # 1

Both Adam and Eve are fully created in the image of God.

Then God said, "Let us make man in our image, in our likeness, and let them rule over the fish of the sea and the birds of the air, over the livestock, over all the earth, and over all the creatures that move along the ground." So God created man in his own image, in the image of God he created him; male and female he created them.

(Genesis 1:26–27)

We start our journey with a straightforward thesis: both male and female human beings were created in God's image. The problem is, older translations of verse 27 say God created "*man*." This whole passage makes more sense in the fairly recent Bible translation, *Today's New International Version* (2001), usually referred to as TNIV, which says, "God created *human beings*." The earlier translations that used "man" are probably responsible for how the idea has stuck all these years that only men were created in the image of God, not women. But read the rest of the verse: "*male and female he created them.*" The Hebrew word often translated as 'man' is more accurately translated as 'human being,' as in TNIV. In Hebrew, the word is *adam*, which simply means 'humanity'—in this case, male humanity and female humanity.

The same sort of confusion could result when reading Genesis 5:1, where most translations say something like, "When God created *man,* he made *him* in the likeness of God. He created *them* male and female; at the time they were created, he blessed *them* and *called them* 'man.'" Again, TNIV clears this up by translating it, "…he blessed them and called them *human beings*." Gilbert Bilezikian puts it this way: "Both man and woman are God's image-bearers" (220).

I

Probably the first time *adam* is used as a personal name is in Genesis 4:25. What is perfectly clear is that two human beings were created—one with male gender and one with female gender—and *both* were created in the image of God.

THESIS # 2

The use of the male pronoun for God does not imply that He is male.

So God created man in his own image, in the image of God he created him.

(Genesis 1:27)

Have you ever tried to imagine what God looks like? Why do most artists portray him as an old man with a long white beard? Jesus told the Samaritan woman that "God is spirit, and his worshipers must worship in spirit and in truth" (John 4:24). So, here's a tough question for you: How do you identify the gender of a *spirit?* If God is pure spirit, he cannot have a body—and how can you tell what gender someone is if there is no body by which to identify the genitalia? That left the Hebrews in a tough position. According to Old Testament scholars, the Hebrew language has no neuter gender (Hess, 80).

Even if the Hebrews had an "it" in their language, it would be wrong to apply neuter gender to a God who had a *personality.* So, being a patriarchal society, they probably decided (or God directed them) to call their God "Him." But by calling both God a "him" and man a "him," one can easily conclude that a "her" must be a lesser category. Interestingly, when God created all the animals, he intentionally created them "male and female." Gender-specific animals require gender-specific pronouns, but the use of the male pronoun for an eternal Spirit-God has sometimes been confusing and misleading.

2

By the way, don't confuse God the Father with the God-man Jesus, even though they are both God. Obviously, before the ever-living Son of God was born into this world, he did not have a body—or genitalia either. And if you wonder why Jesus is referred to as the "Son" of God instead of the "Daughter" or "Child" of God, look at Thesis # 47.

THESIS # 3

Both Adam and Eve receive the identical mandate to rule.

God blessed them and said to them, "Be fruitful and increase in number; fill the earth and subdue it. Rule over the fish in the sea and the birds in the sky and over every living creature that moves on the ground."

(Genesis 1:28 TNIV)

God blessed both the man and the woman and told them *both* to rule (have dominion over) his world. But even in today's society, many people still act as if it's the man's responsibility to be in charge, work and make money while the wife is expected to stay home and tend to the household chores—or in some cases, do all this after she comes home from work! Later in this book, we'll compare what else the Bible says about husband/wife roles. Regardless, when God first created a male and a female *adam* (human being), his command to both of them was identical: "*Rule!* Be in charge of all of my creation."

THESIS # 4

God creates Eve to complement and complete Adam's creation; together they represent male and female reflections of God.

3

The LORD God said, "It is not good for the man to be alone. I will make a helper suitable for him." . . . But for Adam no suitable helper was found.

(Genesis 2:18, 20)

Something very significant seems to be happening here. Four times during the first creation story (Genesis 1), God steps back and looks at what he has done and says, "Good!" (vv. 10, 12, 21 and 25). Then he creates a male and female human being, surveys his work and says, "*Very good!*" (v. 31). However, in chapter 2, the detailed account of how God formed human beings is divided into two parts. After God created Adam, he did not say, "Good." Read v. 18: "The LORD God said it is *not good* for the man to be alone."

Instead of immediately fixing the problem for the man, God asked the man to name all the animals that he (God) had created. The passage may imply that, as the man looked at all of these pairs of animals, he might have asked (a) why was he only one half of a male-female pair, or even (b) would any of those females he had just named make an appropriate partner for him? By now he had probably watched these animals enjoying their male-female differences. We can only imagine that the man felt some sort of void or incompleteness. Even if the man wasn't looking for a partner (which I doubt), God was certainly teaching him that the situation didn't look good! Why? Verse 20 tells us: "But for Adam, *no suitable helper was found.*"

Many devoted Bible scholars think that the reason God created Adam first and permitted him to name the animals before Eve's creation was to show that his position of authority was higher than Eve's. Personally, I side with the authors who suggest that God simply did this to show Adam and Eve that they were *both* uniquely created in the image of God, and that God's mandate to "be fruitful" (1:28) could not be accomplished by Adam without Eve or by Eve without Adam. If God wanted *them* to procreate, it required *both* of them to co-operate.

4

Now, let's go back to where God says he will make a "helper suitable" for Adam (2:18, 20). The term 'helper suitable' is used to translate the Hebrew *etzer kenegdo*, which carries the idea of someone who can appropriately match or correspond to another's need—in this case, Adam's. God did not create Eve to be Adam's servant or under his rule. That kind of hierarchical relationship only appears after sin enters (see 3:20 and Thesis #13). In fact, this "suitable helper" idea is used of God himself several times in the Old Testament. Consider Psalm 46:1: "God is our refuge and strength, an ever-present *help* in trouble." God's help for us is always suitable but never subservient.

Surely, when God meets our needs, he doesn't become some sort of slave or genie at our beck and call. Even the long-established King James Version of the Bible is careful to refer to Eve as a 'help-*meet*'—an early English term that infers complementarity (the idea that they both complement each other). If God had intended Eve to be Adam's servant, seventeenth century translators would probably have used 'help-*mate*' instead, like a second-mate to the captain of a ship. Nothing in this Genesis story suggests that Eve was to be the junior partner in this first male-female relationship.

THESIS # 5

Adam and Eve share the identical physical substance and divine essence.

Then the LORD God formed a man from the dust of the ground and breathed into his nostrils the breath of life, and the man became a living being…So the LORD God caused the man to fall into a deep sleep; and while he was sleeping, he took one of the man's ribs and then closed up the place with flesh. Then the LORD God made a woman from the rib he had taken out of the man, and he brought her to the man.

(Genesis 2:7, 21–22 TNIV)

Genesis 1 plainly describes God making the world, fish, birds, animals, etc. simply by *speaking* (vv. 1–26). God said, "Let there be light!" and there was light! He just spoke and it happened—perhaps instantaneously, perhaps over time, who knows? "Let there be elephants!" "Let there be sheep!" etc. Then we notice a dramatic change in v. 26 (TNIV): "Let us *make* human beings in our image, in our likeness." God didn't just say, "Let there be a man and a woman!" He took the time and skill to hand-make them. The Hebrew word for 'make' is *yatzar*, which suggests artistry or craftsmanship.

In Genesis 2 we learn how Adam was created: (a) God "formed" the man from the dust of the ground and (b) he breathed into his nostrils the breath of life. Apparently, it was only then that the man became a "living being." Once Adam names all the animals and no suitable counterpart is found for him, God uniquely fashions a "female man." But notice, God doesn't use the dust of the earth to create Eve; he uses a rib and some flesh from Adam (vv. 21–22). Obviously, something very special is happening here that did not happen with the other animals. When God made sheep, he didn't take a rib from the ram and make a ewe. What is God possibly trying to teach us?

Over the years, the Christian church—as well as other world religions—has historically portrayed Eve as a much less significant being than Adam because she was created after him. For example, J. David Pawson says, "...woman was created *from, for* and *after* man and was therefore *named* by him" (66-67). It always amazes me that two equally knowledgeable and committed Christians can look at the same verses of Scripture and interpret them differently. In this passage I see a magnificent example of complete equality in the forming of the first man and woman. God seems to go out of his way to ensure that they are both recipients of his personal creative action and his divine presence.

Authors either differ on or ignore the issue of why God only breathed the "breath of life" into Adam. If God wanted to show equality, why did he not just "speak" them both into being, as he did with the animals? Because then they would just be animals. Even if he spoke them into being and then imparted his spiritual essence through his breath (the Hebrew word for 'breath' and 'spirit' is the same), that first couple would still be like the animals, except with a capacity for spiritual things. No, we needed to see a man perfectly created and fully, independently functional, yet now aware of and lonely for the fulfillment that a *unique, independently functional, hand-crafted, equal counterpart* could provide. Eve was not formed out of dust, making her *similar* to Adam's flesh—she *became* Adam's flesh in female form. God did not breathe himself into Eve in a *similar* way to that of Adam—she *became* the same spiritual essence as Adam.

Joy E. Fleming sums it up in one short phrase: "The man and woman will share a common identity without being identical" (10). So does Bilezikian: "From one being, God made two persons" (29). God's presence in physical male now unites with that same presence in physical female in order for them to assume their joint responsibilities as co-regents reigning over his creation.

THESIS # 6

When Adam first sees Eve, he immediately acknowledges them both as "one flesh."

The man said, "This is now bone of my bones and flesh of my flesh; she shall be called 'woman,' for she was taken out of man." For this reason a man will leave his father and mother and be united to his wife, and they will become one flesh. The man and his wife were both naked, and they felt no shame.

(Genesis 2:23–25)

The second chapter of Genesis records the account of one very excited man waking up to see what God had created: a female *adam* (human being). No wonder he is excited—nothing in the animal kingdom he had just named is anything like her! Scholars tell us that the short, simple Hebrew words he uses roughly translate into three brief sentences, or pairs of words, something like, 'This is it!' (or, 'At last!'), 'Bone of my bone!' and 'Flesh of my flesh!' In plain English, it might have gone something like this:

> "Wow! This is certainly not an elephant or sheep. Finally, something looks v-e-r-r-y good! This is exactly what I am! Same bone and flesh as mine.
> "But wait! She's *different* in a very attractive sort of way—this must be a *female-me!* Let's see, I'm an *ish* (Hebrew for man) so that means she must be an *ishshah* (woman)."

Those who think that God gave Adam (men) power and authority over Eve (women) interpret this passage to say, "See, this proves Adam was meant to be the boss because he chose a name for her, just like he did for the animals." Not so fast! The Hebrew word *ish-shah* is not a *name*, it's merely the *feminine form* of *ish*. Ironically, Genesis 3:20 tells us that Adam finally assigned the proper name "Eve" to his wife, with the explanation: "because she would become the mother of all living." Notice, this male-dominant decision only occurs after sin has entered. Ever since, many men have been unwilling to share the throne with their wives.

God didn't handcraft the woman to bring her to the man and say, "Here, Adam. It's not good to see you alone, so I've made you your very own servant. Call her whatever you want. After all, she came *from* you, *after* you and I created her *for* you." I know that sounds very sarcastic, but I also know a lot of men who treat their wives like that— and a lot of women who take it because their pastor told them it's God's plan. But read what the text says next: "For this reason, a man will *leave* his father and mother and be united to his wife, and they will become *one flesh*." God's intention was, and still is, purposeful, peaceful, conjugal unity without losing individuality, a state which only can

8

be realized when a man and woman willingly choose to function as one. As Bilezikian states, "The procedure of a man's separating from his father and cleaving to his wife reflects anything but a patriarchal-dominated society" (34).

The chapter (Genesis 2) ends with a very significant statement: Adam and Eve were naked and "*felt no shame*" (v. 25). We read it so quickly we don't stop to realize the staggering importance of such a statement! In a marriage where the husband and wife genuinely feel equal to each other in every way, there is a transparency and mutual desire to please each other sexually. The unconditional love they receive from each other creates a morally pure, equal, pleasant and secure atmosphere to reciprocate in love. Sadly, in a fallen world, more than one selfish, dominant husband has used this verse to "encourage" his shy, modest wife to try things (sexual or otherwise) far beyond her level of comfort or opinion of Christian morality. Yet, steeped in the headship/submission model, she obeys, even though the feelings of shame, guilt or inadequacy often deepen. In this short little verse, God prepares us for the pain of broken relationships to come after sin enters his perfect world.

THESIS # 7

Perhaps the serpent chooses Eve to tempt because God's command about what not to eat was only given to Adam.

Now the serpent was more crafty than any of the wild animals the LORD God had made. He said to the woman, "Did God really say, 'You must not eat from any tree in the garden'?"

(Genesis 3:1)

Basically, this verse tells us that Satan is very crafty. So, it would be just like him to pounce on the fact that the command not to eat from a certain tree was given from the Lord God to Adam, and only Adam, before Eve was created. The only knowledge Eve had about the tree was whatever Adam told her. Hearing the command from Adam—a mere mortal like herself—may not have had the same awesome impact as if the Lord God had also directly told her.

Why do I mention this? Because Satan is not above using every trick in the book to lead us astray. One can easily imagine his devious explanation to Eve: "God didn't *really* say that, did he? Of course you won't die. He's just protecting you from becoming like him, knowing good and evil" (vv. 1–4). The deceiver comes across sounding so right, so knowledgeable! This point will come up again in the next thesis.

THESIS # 8

Both Adam and Eve bear individual responsibility for disobeying God.

When the woman saw that the fruit of the tree was good for food and pleasing to the eye, and also desirable for gaining wisdom, she took some and ate it. . . . Then the eyes of both of them were opened . . .

(Genesis 3:6–7)

Those who believe the Bible teaches that women are not equal to men often turn to these verses to make their point: Eve ate the forbidden fruit first, then she tempted Adam to eat; therefore she was responsible for his "falling away" from God's perfect sinless plan for all mankind. In fact, theologians still refer to this dramatic incident as "the Fall," and many are still convinced that it was all Eve's fault. Authors O'Faolain and Martines have compiled a fascinating book called *Not in God's Image*, in which they have quoted scores of people who have held this view of women. For instance, Gratian, a twelfth century Italian monk, states that, because Eve led him into "wrongdoing," Adam should have her "under his direction, so that he may not fail a second time through female levity" (130).

But let's remember that Satan (the serpent) specifically tempted the person God *did not directly speak to* (Thesis # 7), using all his scheming expertise to convince her that her interpretation of God's command was all wrong. On the other hand, Adam didn't face Satan at all; he simply decided to go along with Eve. Eve was tricked by the best trickster of all time, but Adam should have known better. I see no biblical evidence that Eve can be accused of causing Adam to sin.

By the way, maybe Eve didn't eat the fruit first. Some scholars point out that the Hebrew word *vav* or *waw,* translated 'and,' can be used either 'concurrently,' as in 'at the same time' (she *and* Adam ate together), or 'consecutively,' as in 'one after the other' (she ate, *then* gave it to Adam). In all probability, Adam was standing beside her through it all. Whether she ate first or they ate together, he still could have refused. If anything, it appears as if Adam bears the greater culpability. The point is, they both sinned, were both responsible, and both suffered the consequences. So it is with us as well. For more on this, see Theses #76 and #77.

THESIS # 9

When confronted by God, Eve openly confesses; Adam makes excuses.

And he said, "Who told you that you were naked? Have you eaten from the tree that I commanded you not to eat from?" The man said, "The woman you put here with me—she gave me some fruit from the tree, and I ate it." Then the LORD God said to the woman, "What is this you have done?" The woman said, "The serpent deceived me, and I ate"

(Genesis 3:11–14)

Many people sincerely believe the Bible teaches that men are better at leadership, at least in spiritual things, than women are. Ironically, many women believe this too. In 1965, Helen Andelin brought out a hugely popular book called *Fascinating Womanhood*. Commenting on the role of men and husbands, she says, "It was God who placed the man at the head of the family and commanded him to earn the bread" (129). Eight years later, Marabel Morgan's controversial book, *The Total Woman*, hit the Christian bookshelves. Morgan's view is that "God planned for woman to be under her husband's rule" (69), apparently because "God ordained man to be the head of the family, its president, and his wife to be the executive vice-president" (70). At the same time, thousands of pastors were echoing the advice Larry Christensen gave in his best-seller, *The Christian Family*, where he argues that "stronger shoulders are given to the man; he has a greater *natural strength of mind*," whereas the heart of a woman "is more easily discouraged and dejected. *God has made her that way*" (127-128, emphasis mine).

Are these people reading the same Bible that I am? When I read Genesis 3, I think Eve comes off looking a lot better than Adam. If I had been searching for a spiritual leader in the Garden of Eden that day, I would have chosen Eve in a heartbeat. Notice how immature Adam appears when God asks him if he has eaten from the tree. Instead of admitting he has sinned, Adam gets defensive: "Don't blame me—it was the woman you put here with me. It's all *her* fault, and *yours*. If you hadn't created her and given her to me, I wouldn't be in this mess now." Is this the same Adam who, before sinning, praised God for her ("At last! This is it!")? Now, compare that to Eve's no-nonsense confession: "The serpent deceived me, and I ate it." Plain and simple. No excuses. No blaming. Guilty as charged.

THESIS # 10

Only Satan and the ground are cursed by God—not Adam and Eve.

So the LORD God said to the serpent, "Because you have done this, Cursed are you . . . " To Adam he said . . . "Cursed is the ground because of you…"

(Genesis 3:14, 17)

As a result of Adam and Eve breaking God's command to not eat from the tree of the knowledge of good and evil, both of them must face ongoing consequences, *but God does not curse them.* The cause-and-effect seems stronger in Adam's case than Eve's, probably because Adam willfully ignored God's command. For this disobedience, God curses the ground (not Adam) for coming generations—the very ground from which Adam was created. As a result, every generation since has suffered the consequences of Adam's disobedience. On the other hand, God's words to Eve read like a "good news/bad news" story. If you look at them in reverse order, God seems to be telling Eve (and all women to come) something like this: "Here's the bad news: having babies will be far more painful from now on. But the good news is that one day another woman will painfully give birth to the One who will destroy Satan" (Genesis 3:15–16).

The main recipient of God's punishment is Satan, who is disguised as a serpent and is the direct cause for God's curse (see v. 14: "Because *you* have done this…"). The condemnation he receives is apparently twofold: he will crawl on his belly and eat dust for the rest of is life, and there will be an ongoing battle between him and Eve (women). This futuristic scene is couched in some pretty high-grade prophetic imagery that probably refers to Satan's final doom through woman's offspring (Christ), who will finally "crush" Satan's head. This is undoubtedly the yet-unfilled prophecy that Mel Gibson chillingly portrays in his film, *The Passion of the Christ*,* as we watch a foot stomp-ing on the head of a snake. But for now, as the old serpent keeps "striking at our heels," we need to understand that neither Adam nor Eve, nor any of us born since, have been cursed by God. Rather, we live each day in an imperfect, fallen world—a consequence of Adam and Eve's choice (see next thesis and compare # 77).

THESIS # 11

Satan is condemned for deceiving the woman, and his ultimate destruction is foretold.

So the LORD *God said to the serpent, "Because you have done this, Cursed are you above all the livestock and all the wild animals! You will crawl on your belly and you will eat dust all the days of your life. And I will put enmity between you and the woman, and between your offspring and hers; he will crush your head, and you will strike his heel."*

(Genesis 3:14–15)

Whatever you think about snakes in general or how you imagine snakes propelled themselves before sin came along, this particular serpent is unique. Without doubt, he is the same one John calls the "ancient serpent," or Satan, twice in the book of Revelation (12:9; 20:2). God places two devastating but justified curses on him—one to take effect immediately, the other at the end of the world (see pre-vious Thesis # 10).

Both Adam and Eve are given opportunity to state their case, and both do so. However, God doesn't let Satan say anything. As soon as Eve confesses ("The serpent deceived me and I ate."), God addresses the serpent: "Because you have done *this*, here is my curse upon you." One can assume the "this" refers to Satan deceiving Eve. How sad,

---

* Gibson, Mel (Director and Co-producer). (2004). *The Passion of the Christ*. United States: Newmarket Films.

then, that so many Christian authors through the years view Eve and/or all women as satanic or impure, deserving of condemnation because she (they) caused Adam (men) to sin.

Just as Satan's curse has two stages, so does God's declaration (not curse) to Eve. First, God says, "I will make your pains in childbearing very severe; with pain you will give birth to children" (Genesis 3:16 TNIV). Maybe this is God's way of assuring Eve that his original mandate to "be fruitful and multiply" has not changed. Regarding the second stage, one can only wonder if Eve understood the prophetic words about Satan finally being crushed by one of her descendents, but from our vantage point, it is an amazing statement of grace!

God could have cursed Eve for her sin (many others have over the years!) and said, "Eve, because you have done this, you no longer deserve to be co-ruler with Adam. From now on, men will take the leadership role. Women will be inferior to men and will be denied positions of authority and leadership, especially in spiritual matters." But God does not put Eve down, nor does he curse the ground because of her. Instead, he gives her reassurance that she and her seed will play a very significant role in his new-world order.

THESIS # 12

Adam's sin is not in the act of listening to his wife, but in disobeying God.

To Adam he said, "Because you listened to your wife and ate from the tree about which I commanded you, 'You must not eat of it' . . . "

(Genesis 3:17)

If you are convinced that women should never take leadership roles in church settings, you will probably agree with Ray Ortlund, who has written that Adam sinned by listening to Eve: "He abandoned his headship...this moral failure in Adam led to his ruination" (110). Pawson goes even further, stating that "In taking a 'feminine role,' Adam was abdicating his position" (24). Such statements can easily become grounds to condemn Eve for causing Adam to sin and, consequently, restrict all women for all time from leading or teaching men. That's why Pawson and others will not ordain women or let them be elders, etc. Consider what he says about Eve: "Her assuming the role of leadership had disastrous consequences *and must not be followed by other women*" (75, emphasis mine).

Yes, God said, "Because you listened to your wife..." but the sentence doesn't stop there. I'm fairly sure God would not have minded if Adam had listened to *good* advice from Eve. The sin in question here is not men listening to their wives, or wives being so bold that they share their opinions with their husbands, it is that *after* Adam listened to her, he chose an action that was directly contrary to the command that an Almighty God had previously addressed to *him*.

THESIS # 13

Adam's dominance and Eve's submission sadly describe reality in a fallen world.

"Your desire will be for your husband, and he will rule over you"

(Genesis 3:16)

The second half of v. 16 strikes me as one of the saddest verses in the Bible. Every time I read it, I think of the thousands of couples I have counselled. Over and over, this short declaration succinctly sums up so many dysfunctional marriages: *"Your desire will be for your husband, and he will rule over you."*

The second chapter of Genesis ends with celebration and jubilation as both Adam and Eve revel in the joy of a perfect, harmonious, reciprocal one-flesh union. Then sin enters and brings with it lust, pride, ambition, dominance, manipulation, lies and dysfunction. It was terrible for both of them! For Adam, the joy of tending a perfect garden is replaced with back-breaking labor, thistles, lost communication with God and the ever-present fear of death. In the beginning they shared authority and companionship—Eve was always part of the solution—but now Adam works alone and receives very little sympathy from her. With no other tools at his disposal, how easy it is to begin imposing his greater physical strength to command and intimidate.

For Eve, the memories of passionate, tender moments together with her lover are replaced with unrequited love. She longs to have her lover back, but only gets an angry, selfish stranger who is unable, or unwilling, to tenderly treat her as an equal. It is not surprising that Bilezikian (267) and Fleming (40) both include a haunting quotation by then Harvard Divinity School Ph.D. candidate Carol Castor Howard, as she describes the grim reality: *"The woman wants a mate and she gets a master; she wants a lover and she gets a lord; she wants a husband and she gets a hierarch."*

Surely, this cannot be what God intended. So, what must we conclude? It is painfully apparent that God's words to Eve in Genesis 3:16 are not meant to be a *decree of how things should be* after the Fall, but rather a *description of how things would be* because of the Fall.

THESIS # 14

Many women in the Old Testament capably serve God in prominent, authoritative leadership roles.

(Exodus 15; Judges 4; 2 Kings 22; 2 Chronicles 34)

People who are convinced that women should not be in positions of spiritual leadership are often at a loss to explain why God used many outstanding women as leaders in the Old Testament. Many of the bravest, holiest and most talented servants of God mentioned in the Bible were women who often put the best reigning or anointed men of the day to shame. Let's briefly look at a few of them.

Miriam (Exodus 15)

Even as a young child, this Hebrew girl seems to show leadership and responsibility. Exodus 2:4 gives the impression that it was her idea to watch out for her baby brother Moses when their mother hid him in the in the basket-boat. When Pharaoh's daughter found Moses, it was Miriam who stepped up to recommend a "nurse" for the baby—Moses' mother, actually. (If young David had done what Miriam did, it would no doubt have been referred to as a sign of his future potential leadership capabilities once he became a *man*). Now, fast-forward to Exodus 15:20 and meet who the author calls *Miriam the prophet* (TNIV). *She* is leading the other women in a song she has just composed: "Sing to the LORD, for he is highly exalted…" (v. 21). Years later, the prophet Micah reminds the Israelites of what God said about this woman's contribution to their history: "I sent Moses to lead you, also Aaron and *Miriam*." In other words, "I sent you three leaders: Moses, Aaron and Miriam."

Deborah (Judges 4)

Judges 4:4 (TNIV) says, "Now Deborah, a prophet, the wife of Lappidoth, was leading Israel at that time." It doesn't say "…the wife of Lappidoth *who* was leading Israel at that time." Deborah is not married to a prophet-judge who is leading Israel—she *is* the prophet-judge, and *she* is leading Israel. As far as we know from Scripture, only she and Samuel held both the position of prophet and judge. This is groundbreaking news on three counts: (a) a *woman* is called a prophet; (b) the story is about *her*, not her husband; and (c) a *woman* is leading the Israelites! For forty years, Deborah holds court every day and all the Israelites take the difficult cases to *her*. But wait! The best part of the story is when Israel's five-star general refuses to lead the troops into war *unless she goes with him* (Judges 4:8). As Grady points out, she "presents an intriguing problem" for today's churches who won't recognize that women can lead men as well (37).

Huldah (2 Kings 22, 2 Chronicles 34)

The Israelites had stopped following God's "Book of the Law" for a generation or so until one day Hilkiah the priest stumbled across a copy of it and sent his secretary to Josiah the king. When the king heard the content of it, he told Hilkiah and three others to "Go and inquire of the LORD" (v. 13). Now, here's where the story took an unexpected twist. Verse 14 tells us that the four of them "went to speak to the *prophet* Huldah"! What follows is this woman's scathing prophecy to Israel, punctuated three times by the authoritative *"This is what the LORD says!"* The result was a serious, widespread revival that caused all of Israel to smash their false gods and return to the one true Lord God. The chapter goes on to record, "Neither before nor after Josiah was there a king like him who turned to the LORD as he did" (2 Kings 23:25). All because of a *woman's* prophecy!

Can you say that all of these women were out of God's will? If you think it is unbiblical for women to be spiritual leaders, how do you account for these three outstanding women? Years ahead of his time, George Fox (1624–91), founder of the Society of Friends, or Quakers, ensured that English Quaker women were welcomed as priests, elders and teachers. O'Faolain and Martines have recorded several excerpts where Fox states that, after the Fall, women and men were brought back into the image of God through "restoration by Christ," now qualifying such women to speak and become elders in the church (266).

THESIS # 15

The composite "Proverbs 31 Woman" challenges traditional male-female stereotypes.

She selects wool and flax and works with eager hands. She is like the merchant ships, bringing her food from afar. She gets up while it is still night. . . . She considers a field and buys it; out of her earnings she plants a vineyard. . . . She makes linen garments and sells them, and supplies the merchants with sashes.

(selections from Proverbs 31:13–24 TNIV)

Our somewhat subjective choice of gender-equal sections of the Bible causes us to jump ahead to the book of Proverbs. This is a great spot to recommend J. Lee Grady's "must-read" book, *Ten Lies the Church Tells Women.* In his "Lie # 9," called "Women shouldn't work outside the home" (it's a "lie," remember), he reviews what the Old and New Testaments say about women working both in and out of the home setting. Although no one woman could possibly do all the activities mentioned in Proverbs 31, the point is that one could be a good mother while still excelling in any one or more of these male-defined tasks. Grady also reminds us that, before the Industrial Revolution of the 1800s, most women worked alongside their husbands, often with older children and extended family members looking after the young ones (158).

Of course, all of this flies in the face of historical stereotyping. For instance, look at a few of the best-selling Christian authors in the '60s and '70s. Remember Helen Andelin from Thesis #9? She reminds women to not "hash things over as men do," because that places women on an equal plane with men: "Remember, in giving a man advice, keep him in the dominant position so that he will feel needed and adequate as the leader" (145). You also met Marabel Morgan in Thesis # 9, who writes, "God planned for woman to be under her husband's rule" (69). Finally, Larry Christensen reinforces this on page after page of *The Christian Family*, where he states the danger of the "blurring of mother–father roles" and the "departure from 'Divine order'" (45). The popularity of these books among average Christian homes during that era left a profound impact. Sadly, scores of other church leaders and authors were—and still are— saying the same thing.

Perhaps my favorite part of this chapter in Proverbs is vv. 25–26: "*She is clothed with strength and dignity; she can laugh at the days to come. She speaks with wisdom, and faithful instruction is on her tongue.*" I have a hunch that if these words were said of a *man* in the Bible, everyone would applaud his leadership skills and promote him to a high office in the church.

THESIS # 16

The Song of Songs is a delightful poetic example of how God intends married couples to reciprocally enjoy sex.

His left arm is under my head, and his right arm embraces me. . . . Daughters of Jerusalem, I charge you by the gazelles and by the does of the field: Do not arouse or awaken love until it so desires.

(Song of Songs 2:6; 3:5)

Hundreds of books and articles basically cover the same topics as I am addressing in this book, but very few of them mention a little book in the Old Testament sandwiched between Ecclesiastes and Isaiah called The Song of Songs (some translations call it The Song of Solomon). Historically, it has been drummed into most Christians that this book is meant to be a story, or allegory, describing Christ's love-relationship with the church. I'm thankful that most modern scholars consider it to be what it sounds like on first reading—a stylized, poetic manual on love-making, which may or may not have secondary or prophetic reference to Christ.

In my private marriage counseling practice, I use this book as much as any other part of the Bible. I suggest to some couples that they read certain sections together, then try to compose similar personalized "love-poems" to each other. Frankly, if every married couple spoke to each other the way the "lover" and the "beloved" do in this book, most marriage counselors would be out of a job. And it wouldn't hurt if every couple bought James Dillow's excellent book, *Solomon on Sex*.

In 1:2 the woman ecstatically tells her lover, "Your love is more delightful than wine." No dominant, demanding male partner here! The chapter ends with parallel admiration for each other—first him to her: "How beautiful you are, my darling! Oh, how beautiful," followed by her to him: "How handsome you are my lover! Oh, how charming!"

The other seven chapters are drenched with much "adult-accompaniment"-sounding love-poems, not unlike verbal foreplay, graphically describing the unbridled infatuation of one for the other. I enjoy reading how the woman responds to the man after hearing his poem: "My beloved is mine and I am his" (2:16 TNIV). Note the equality, as well as her closing announcement to all the daughters of Jerusalem: *"This is my beloved, this is my friend…"* (5:16 TNIV).

Finally, look at the short command that is repeated *three times* in these eight short chapters: *"Do not arouse or awaken love until it so desires"* (2:7; 3:5; 8:4). I see nothing in this entire book that would suggest anything less than total gender equality in relation to a couple's love-making. If an equal, reciprocal couple can experience even greater than average pleasure in the *bedroom* without the male "in charge" or taking the initiative, why must men be in charge in other rooms in the house, or in the *church*?

THESIS # 17

God purposely chooses to unite his son's deity with humanity by the use of a woman's womb.

"Joseph son of David, do not be afraid to take Mary home as your wife, because what is conceived in her is from the Holy Spirit. She will give birth to a son, and you are to give him the name Jesus, because he will save his people from their sins.

(Matthew 1:20–21)

In Matthew, we find the first of two accounts of the birth of Jesus; the second is in the first two chapters of Luke. Matthew tells us that while Mary, the young mother-to-be, was "pledged" to a man named Joseph, they find out that she's pregnant—but they've never had sex. After Joseph considers divorcing her but decides against it, he has a dream in which an angel explains what has really happened: "What is conceived in her is from the Holy Spirit" (v. 20). He tells Joseph that the son she's carrying is to be called Jesus, "because he will save his people from their sins" (v. 21).

The account in Luke's gospel is far more detailed. Here, the angel comes to Mary with the same story: she will have a baby and is to name him Jesus. When Mary asks how this will happen, the angel explains, "The Holy Spirit will come upon you, and the power of the Most High will overshadow you. So the holy one to be born will be called the Son of God" (Luke 1:34–36). Upon hearing that her cousin Elizabeth is also six months pregnant with a miraculous baby (John), Mary goes to visit her. Convinced by now that this whole situation is ordained by God, Mary composes a poem of praise (Luke 1:46–55), in which she exclaims that God "has been mindful of the humble state of his servant. *From now on all generations will call me blessed"*(v. 48).

Something very profound is going on here. The God who created the universe is about to miraculously form a physical body for his eternal Son, the Messiah—and he is going to use a young virgin to be the vessel! Why didn't God just create a new body out of dust, the way he did for Adam? If women are as sinful and unreliable as history implies, why would he let his Son come into the world that way? Catholic nun and author Joan Chittister captures the impact of the moment in her book, *Heart of Flesh:* "The Jesus born of a woman without the agency of a man defies in that very generation all the dualism, hierarchy, domination and inequality practiced in his name" (p. 25).

THESIS # 18

The primary requirement for Christian leaders is that they function as servants.

"You know that the rulers of the Gentiles lord it over them, and their high officials exercise authority over them. Not so with you."

(Matthew 20:25–26)

"Now that I, your Lord and Teacher, have washed your feet, you also should wash one another's feet."

(John 13:14)

In Matthew 20:21, the mother of Zebedee's sons just didn't get it. "Why can't my two sons sit on both sides of the Christ when he reigns in his kingdom?" Wouldn't any mother want that for her sons? In John 13:6–8 Peter doesn't get it either: "Lord, what are you *doing?* No, I *won't* let you wash my feet. It's wrong! It just isn't *done!*"

To really get the impact of what's happening in these two stories, look them up in your Bible. Simply put, both of these well-meaning followers of Jesus had a this-world concept of leadership and authority, which says, "My main goal in life is for my children to become leaders who people will respect and look up to. Then they won't get pushed around and treated like slaves." That's why Peter just couldn't get his head around his *Lord* actually washing his feet—"That's a slave-job!" Even today, we live in a dog-eat-dog society where the "Man at the Top," the "Head Honcho," the cold, calculating "Alpha Dog" is considered the epitome of what leadership should be. And, obviously, tough he-man types are much more suited for such a position than women.

Jesus scathingly chides the religious leaders of his day for how they "lord it over" the Gentiles, then addresses the disciples with clarity and brevity: *"Not so with you!"* Or, as the KJV has it: "But it shall not be so among you." Jesus seems to be saying, "My plan for all of you is that you become *servants*. It's that simple. You're all on the same level. In my church, none of you can be lords or masters. In the church of Jesus Christ, there is only one Master. Your role, if you choose to accept it, is to be a servant."

I deeply appreciate Gilbert Bilezikian. If you haven't ordered your copy of *Beyond Sex Roles* yet, please do it now. But until it comes, consider these two quotations of his.

> In a society intoxicated with the spirit of competition and driven by upward mobility obsessions, Jesus establishes a community of disciples who seek the status of servants and who aspire to downward mobility, so as to make themselves available to each other in sacrificial service and devote themselves to the fulfillment of the needs of others (110)....Jesus taught His followers in word and deed to consider the gender difference irrelevant to the concerns and to the processes of the kingdom of God (118).

Such radical teaching begs the question: If the primary requirement for leadership is for a person to be a servant, then why can't women fill the role of servant-leader just as well as men? They've certainly been practicing the servant-role for long enough.

THESIS # 19

The woman who pours costly perfume on Jesus' head is immortalized in Scripture.

"Truly I tell you, wherever this gospel is preached throughout the world, what she has done will also be told, in memory of her."

(Matthew 26:13; Mark 14:9 TNIV)

In this story—recorded not just once, but in two of the gospels—we encounter a woman who stands in stark contrast to the disciples in the last thesis (who either wanted to be important themselves, or just couldn't imagine Jesus doing menial tasks). We know her as Mary, the sister of Lazarus; yet in both accounts she remains nondescript and unnamed. Without a word, she quietly approaches Jesus while he and his disciples are eating (she probably cooked the meal!), opens a little jar of perfume and anoints her Savior's head.

Does that sounds like a story worth seven verses in Matthew and another seven in Mark? Actually, the disciples didn't consider it important either (Matthew 26:8–9): "What a waste! That stuff must have cost a whole year's wages. Why didn't she sell the perfume and give the money to the poor? Come to think of it, why did Jesus let her do this?" Such questions are to be expected from administrative executives. Secular leadership would see only the fiscal irresponsibility. But Jesus saw it differently: "Why are you bothering this woman? She has done a beautiful thing to me" (v. 10). No doubt, the indignant disciples learned an unforgettable lesson as Jesus added, "I tell you the truth, wherever this gospel is preached throughout the world, what she has done will also be told, in memory of her" (v. 13).

THESIS # 20

Women are the first to witnesses Christ's resurrection, and are sent by him to announce the good news to the apostles.

"You are looking for Jesus the Nazarene, who was crucified. He has risen! . . . But go, tell his disciples and Peter, 'He is going ahead of you into Galilee. There you will see him, just as he told you.'"

(Mark 16:6–7)

Why did Jesus choose the particular men he did to be his disciples? What an amazing privilege to be one of his twelve hand-picked men—and then to get the benefit of three years of quality time with and life-changing teaching from the Messiah himself! Surely, at the end of that one-of-a-kind seminary course, they'd be ready for any spiritual battle, wouldn't they? But the writers of the first four books of the New Testament (two of whom were apostles) paint a very different picture. Not that all of them were traitors, like Judas, but neither were they shining examples of obedience and commitment to their Savior. In any church today, I'm not sure they'd even be chosen for a deacon or elder position—and you sure wouldn't want Judas taking up the offering!

But Jesus knew all this; he even foretold it. After spending his last intimate supper with his disciples, he announces, "This very night you will all fall away on account of me" (Matthew 26:31), warning them of what to expect after the crucifixion and resurrection: *"But after I have risen, I will go ahead of you into Galilee"* (v. 32). Upon hearing this grim prediction, Peter is the first to boldly state, "'Even if I have to die with you, I will never disown you.' And all the other disciples said the same thing" (v. 35). But by the time the soldiers arrest Jesus, we read of no evidence of the disciples' commitment to their Savior, only the statement, "Then all the disciples deserted him and fled" (Matthew 26:56).

I find something very puzzling here. If you had been told by Jesus that he would *come back to life and go before you into Galilee*, don't you think it just might cross your mind Sunday morning when you wake up—*to go to Galilee*? Even if you weren't quite sure he was the Christ and just might rise from the dead, what harm would there be in checking it out? At least, it might be a nice gesture for you to wake up your buddy disciples and all drop in at the tomb to grieve his death. That's exactly what the women did (the two Marys, Joanna, Salome and maybe others). It was the least they could do: give their Lord the proper burial protocol he deserved.

Next morning. Women at the tomb. Stone "door" is rolled back. Empty tomb! An angel explains that Jesus has risen, and tells them, "Go quickly and tell his disciples: 'He has risen from the dead and is going ahead of you *into Galilee. There you will see him*' " (Matthew 28:7). Later, Jesus tells them the same thing: "Go and tell my brothers to go *to Galilee; there they will see me.*" When the women relay this message to the apostles, they simply don't believe them, because "their words seemed to them like nonsense" (Luke 24:11).

They're disciples, for goodness sake—and they still don't get it. Peter deserves some credit—at least he went to look into the empty tomb, but then went away, "wondering to himself what had happened" (v. 12). Apparently, it was only the apprehensive and fearful women who were convinced "He really is alive!" So Jesus commissions them to tell the disciples.

Mathew 28:16 records that the eleven disciples went to Galilee, exactly "where Jesus had told them to go." What a novel idea! Maybe I'm reading too much into this story, but please take a minute to think through these questions.

(a) Who do you *really* think handled Christ's crucifixion and resurrection better—the apostles Jesus called and taught for three

years, or the few untrained women he commissioned to announce the best news the world has ever heard?

(b) Who showed the greater faith and obedience—the twelve Jesus explicitly told he would go to Galilee after his resurrection, or the women he sent to tell (remind?) the disciples to go to Galilee?

(c) If Jesus really believed and taught that important ministry assignments should only be given to men, why didn't he find four or five men to announce the good news to the other disciples? Would the disciples have been more inclined to believe men than women?

Every reader should begin to consider that there just *may* be nothing genetically or spiritually built into maleness that would automatically make men better Christian leaders than women.

THESIS # 21

Jesus shatters historical, cultural and religious protocol by privately conversing with a Samaritan woman.

When a Samaritan woman came to draw water, Jesus said to her, "Will you give me a drink?"

(John 4:7)

The account of "The Woman At the Well" (John 4:4-26) is one of the better-known Sunday school stories. Jesus knows that to get from Judea to Galiee he has to go through Samaria—"enemy territory" to Jews. At noon, Jesus arrives at a town named Sychar, where he rests at "Jacob's Well." A Samaritan woman comes to the well and Jesus asks her for a drink. Now, notice the significance of what is going on. This is Jesus, the Son of God, who is by now a well-known Jewish teacher, and we find him (a) in Samaria, where no self-respecting Jew would be found, (b) all alone with a Samaritan *woman,* and (c) he is *talking to her* and (d) asking her for a *drink!* Even the woman is surprised: "How can you, a Jew, ask me, a Samaritan woman, for a drink?" (4:9). John further explains, "For Jews do not associate with Samaritans." In fact, Jesus goes beyond associating with her; he takes a drink from her cup or jug, and invites her to partake of "living water" (that is, everlasting life)—which, apparently, she does. At this point, the disciples return, surprised to find him "talking with a *woman*" (v. 27). But the grateful woman runs back to her friends and invites them to hear the good news from this man, saying, "Could this be the Messiah?" Verse 30 states that many of them came out from the town to hear Jesus.

The male religious leaders, both Jewish and Samaritan, would have condemned what Jesus had done. It's against the Law! But, as often before, Jesus sets protocol aside and allows an outcast woman from a detested race to not only enjoy salvation, but also to physically minister to him and proclaim the good news to others. As he had explained earlier, "Do not think that I have come to abolish the Law or the Prophets; I have not come to abolish them but to fulfill them" (Matthew 5:17). Ironically, the woman left both filled and fulfilled—which is more than many women (or men, for that matter) feel in some Christian congregations today.

THESIS # 22

The woman caught in the act of adultery, who would have been stoned under the Law, is not condemned by Jesus.

"Let any one of you who is without sin be the first to throw a stone at her."… "Then neither do I condemn you," Jesus declared. "Go now and leave your life of sin."

(John 8:7, 11 TNIV)

Many early manuscripts did not include this story. In some newer Bibles, chapter 8 of John begins with v. 12 and puts this account in a footnote. Whether or not it is supposed to be in the Bible, it is, nevertheless, a good example of the way Jesus championed the cause of women.

The story goes like this: the Jewish teachers of the law and the super-conservative Pharisees of that day just happen to find a woman "caught in the act of adultery" and parade her before Jesus and his group of followers. In an attempt to trap Jesus, these self-righteous zealots haughtily state, "In the Law Moses commanded us to stone such women. Now what do you say?" (v. 5). In other words, "Gotcha!" At this, the ever-compassionate Savior bends down and scribbles something in the sand (will we ever know what?) and utters one of his most famous lines, "If any one of you is without sin, let him be the first to throw a stone at her." The crowd leaves.

Are you looking for a good contrast between Old Testament legalism and Jesus? It doesn't get any better than this. These zealous, hypocritical leaders are willing to shame and stone a contrite, sinning woman because "The letter of the Law is more important! We've been chosen by God! We're right!" The law they refer to is probably Leviticus 20:10: "If a man commits adultery with another man's wife . . . both the adulterer and the adulteress are to be put to death." Did you notice that the equally guilty man in this crime is not even mentioned? How convenient of the Pharisees to point out only that the law commands them to stone such *women* (v. 5). Did you ever wonder about the guy? Did they let him run away? Did they forgive his sin because he was overcome by some satanic seductress?

In characteristic form, Jesus cuts through their double standard. Speechless and guilty, they all leave—all, that is, *except the woman*! The woman who, moments before, trembled in shame as she awaited her inevitable sentence of public stoning before a gawking crowd, now stands still. After all, why should she leave? For the first time in her life, she basks in the acceptance of a forgiving and equalizing God whose compassionate counsel is simply, "Go now and leave your life of sin."

Does your church have a double standard for male/female qualifications for ministry? Do we continue to limit women's ministry because "The Bible says!" while allowing sinful men to be fully redeemed and equipped for any service?

THESIS # 23

The Spirit-filling at Pentecost ushers in unlimited ministries for all believers, regardless of gender, class or race.

"In the last days, God says, I will pour out my Spirit on all people. Your sons and daughters will prophesy, your young men will see visions, your old men will dream dreams. Even on my servants, both men and women, I will pour out my Spirit in those days."

(Acts 2:17–18; Joel 2:28–29)

There's nothing in the Bible quite like Acts 2. Earlier in the book, the author, Luke, says that, just before returning to heaven, Jesus told his followers, "You will receive power when the Holy Spirit comes on you; and you will be my witnesses in Jerusalem, and in all Judea and Samaria, and to the ends of the earth" (Acts 1:8). The incredible happenings in the next chapter are the fulfillment of this prophecy—on the very day that the Jews call the Feast of Pentecost or Feast of Weeks, a very important Jewish feast day (Exodus 34:22). Once a year, Jerusalem played host to visiting Jews "from every nation under Heaven" (Acts 2:5), people of mixed background who spoke many different languages. There could never be a better or larger stage on which to introduce the Holy Spirit. The account describes how the crowd heard a sound like rushing wind, then saw what looked like tongues of fire on everyone's head (2:6–13). Then *all* of them began to hear strangers fluently speaking *their* language. I can imagine the confusion: "What is this?" "I'm afraid." "They must either be crazy or drunk!"

As amazing as all this sounds, the next part is even more amazing. Another *miracle*—Peter steps up and starts *preaching!* That's right, the same impetuous fisherman who promised to never deny his Lord moments before he denied his Lord. This can't be the same man, can it? Well, not quite the same. There is one gigantic difference: the Holy Spirit is living i*n* him and talking *through* him. With a barn-burner of a sermon the crowd will never forget, Peter convincingly explains that this is what the Old Testament prophet Joel had predicted hundreds of years before (Joel 2:28–32). From that moment on, the world could never be the same.

This whole chapter of Acts is the foundation for many different theological and denominational interpretations, and I'm not going to get into them. But, for our purposes, I see two very important changes that took place on that particular Day of Pentecost, changes that are meant to continue until Jesus makes another trip back to planet earth. First, look at the change in Peter's life once the Holy Spirit is in charge. Here's proof positive that God can take an immature, undisciplined fisherman and turn him into the Billy Graham of his day. Peter was not one bit smarter or more experienced when he preached on that day of Pentecost than he was the day before. God didn't choose him because of his phenomenal knowledge or preaching abilities. All God needed was a willing vessel; the Holy Spirit did the rest. And he still does.

Pentecost brought another radical change. Read how Peter explains what an Old Testament preacher named Joel was talking about: "In the last days, God says, I will pour out my Spirit on all people. Your sons and *daughters* will prophesy, your young men will see visions, your old men will dream dreams. Even on my servants, both men and *women*, I will pour out my Spirit in those days, and they will prophesy" (Acts 2:17–18, compare with Joel 2:28–29). Imagine,

Christian men *and* women all receiving the same Holy Spirit (just as they all *spoke or heard tongues* moments before) and all prophesying (or, at least, able to).

As I understand this, God is not saying that now women are *finally* allowed to prophesy—we've already shown that there were women prophets in the Old Testament, but it was the exception then—now it becomes the norm. Neither is God saying, "Here's my new plan: from now on I will occasionally find a talented woman whom I will indwell and commission to preach my Word," nor is he saying that from now on all Christians will automatically make excellent preachers.

So, what is He saying? "*People* of Israel (v. 22 as in TNIV) and others present, let what has happened here today be a strong sign to you. My Son *has been* with some of you. But from now on, my Spirit will *indwell all* of you, male and female (see John 14:17), if you repent and confess my Son as Lord. Then I will empower and gift you, male and female, to prophesy (preach) or perform any other ministry I choose."

Does that sound too radical? Ironically, many biblical scholars are still convinced that it's wrong for women to teach, preach or lead in church meetings—as if teaching, preaching and leadership are abilities God only injected into the DNA of *men*, and women just weren't given that chromosome. Maybe you also hold this "hierarchical" view, but didn't know what it was called. It simply describes those who feel there is a hierarchy in creation, often diagrammed by a top-down prioritized list: (1) God, (2) Christ, (3) man, (4) woman. If you really want to know more about the hierarchical way of interpreting the Bible in relation to gender, read a 565-page book edited by John Piper and Wayne Grudem, titled *Recovering Biblical Manhood and Womanhood*. Their book is probably the most comprehensive and scholarly collection of articles ever published from a hierarchical point of view. Several times they make summary statements like this: "We are persuaded that the Bible teaches that only men should be pastors and elders. That is, men should bear *primary* responsibility for Christ-like leadership and teaching in the church. So it is unbiblical, we believe, and therefore detrimental, for women to assume this role" (60-61).

Pentecost, however, raises some serious problems with their position. How does one account for many women whose obvious gift is preaching? Or why should a church always choose a less-gifted man to preach when there are several gifted women in the same church? Oh, some say, God can empower the man and make up for his shortcomings. Of course he can, and he did it for Peter. But why can he not do the same for a woman? Nothing in this passage suggests that women receive lesser gifts than men. The text is pretty simple— all means *all*.

THESIS # 24

Peter's "Sheet Vision" nullifies Jewish food laws, making all people equal through Christ.

"Do not call anything impure that God has made clean."

(Acts 10:15)

What can we learn about gender equality from a sheet full of unclean animals? Quite a lot—especially if by "unclean" we mean that Jews couldn't eat them, and the person having the dream is a Jew called Peter. In Acts 10, while Peter is sleeping, God sends down a sort of "show and tell" sheet filled with all kinds of wildlife that Jews were forbidden to eat, according to their God-given laws. A voice out of nowhere says, "Get up, Peter. Kill and eat" (v. 13). Peter responds in typical Jewish fashion: "Surely not, Lord. I have never eaten anything impure or unclean." This scenario is repeated three times, and the sheet goes back up to heaven (v. 16).

Peter stays awake, "wondering" and "thinking" (NIV): "What *was* that? What is God trying to tell me?" Next, God tells him that there are three strangers at the door looking for him, and that he should go downstairs and go with them. Can you imagine what he must have been saying to himself? "Let me see now…three times God tells me to eat things Jews can't eat, then he tells me to hang out with three *Gentiles*. Now they want me to come to their *house*. That's even worse than eating forbidden food!"

In our society today, we can't begin to appreciate what a colossal change is taking place here. For thousands of years, God told his chosen people to stay to themselves and live by certain iron-clad rules. Then, within twenty-four hours, everything sacred is changed! Peter, a devout *Jewish* Christian in the home of Cornelius, a *Roman* soldier and follower of Christ, in the *Roman* city of Caesarea, is surrounded by an eager crowd of *Gentile* believers! Before his very eyes, the walls of centuries crumble, and Peter delivers another Spirit-filled sermon: "You are well aware that it is against our law for a Jew to associate with a Gentile or visit him. But God has shown me that I should not call any man impure or unclean" (Acts 10:28). At the end of his sermon, Peter concludes, "I now realize how true it is that God does not show favoritism but accepts men [TNIV says "those"] from every nation who fear him and do what is right" (vv. 34–35).

The impact of this vision on Peter is comparable to that of Paul's experience in Romans 14:14: "As one who *is in the Lord Jesus*, I am fully convinced that no food is unclean *in itself*. But if anyone *regards* something as unclean, then for him it is unclean." For both Peter and Paul the growing appreciation of acceptance *in the Lord Jesus* causes them to regard entrenched legalistic practices in a new and liberating light.

Matthew Henry's Commentary, first published back in 1708, said some interesting things about Peter's vision. Commenting on Acts 15:11, Henry writes: "He that made the law *might alter it when he pleased and reduce the matter to its first state*" (emphasis mine). He goes on to say,

"Ceremonial characters were abolished, that more regard might be had to moral ones." We who promote gender equality feel that before Adam and Eve sinned, they were both completely equal and were jointly commanded to jointly rule this earth. Male dominance and female submission are natural consequences of the Fall, not a new decree from God. The work of Christ enables everyone within the "subculture" of Christianity to return "to its first state." More on this in Thesis # 46.

In Acts 11 Peter goes up to Jerusalem and explains his sheet-vision to the "circumcised believers." Imagine their shock to hear him say, "So, if God gave them [the Gentiles] the same [Holy Spirit] gift as he gave us, who *believed* in the Lord Jesus Christ, who was I to think that I could oppose God?" (11:17). Notice, the only requirement for anyone to receive any gift from the Spirit is *belief in the Lord Jesus Christ*. Through the Spirit guiding us from within, we can now be governed by morals, not ceremony. If God can erase the dividing wall between Jews and Gentiles, surely he can do the same for men and women to return things "to its first state."

THESIS #25

The consistent listing of Priscilla's name before Aquila's probably implies her greater spiritual role.

He [Paul] began to speak boldly in the synagogue. When Priscilla and Aquila heard him, they invited him to their home and explained to him the way of God more adequately.

(Acts 18:26)

How do you address your Christmas cards to married couples? Probably, "Mr. and Mrs.," right? Do you ever write, "Mrs. and Mr.?" Or perhaps, "Pauline and Andrew?" It's rare—even in our gender-sensitive society today—but that's exactly what the New Testament authors do with Priscilla and Aquila. Every time they're mentioned as a couple, Priscilla's name comes first (Except in Acts 18:2, where Priscilla shows up later in the sentence). Look at Acts 18:18. Paul leaves Corinth and sails to Syria "accompanied by Priscilla and Aquila." Verse 19 states that, in Ephesus, Paul left "Priscilla and Aquila." Then in verses 24–25 Paul mentions Apollos, a highly educated man who knew and taught the Scriptures, but "knew only the baptism of John" (not Jesus). When Priscilla and Aquila hear Apollos speaking boldly in the synagogue, they invite him home and explain to him "the way of God more adequately" (v. 26). The positioning of the names makes it almost certain that she was the leader and primary teacher, and the rest of Scripture says nothing that would indicate otherwise.

The Priscilla-first habit appears twice more in the New Testament. In Romans 16, Paul asks the Roman recipients of his letter to greet Priscilla and Aquila, his *fellow workers* in Christ, who both risked their lives for him, and mentions that "all the churches of the Gentiles are grateful to them." He also sends greetings to the church "that meets at *their* house (v. 5). Then, in 2 Timothy 4:19, Paul does it again: "Greet Priscilla and Aquila and the household of Onesiphorus."

THESIS # 26

The spiritual renewing of one's mind qualifies any man or woman to exercise any spiritual gift that God imparts.

Do not conform any longer to the pattern of this world, but be transformed by the renewing of your mind. Then you will be able to test and approve what God's will is—his good, pleasing and perfect will.

(Romans 12:2)

The twelfth chapter of Romans demands a lot from Christian "brothers and sisters" (as TNIV translates v. 1). It begins by urging us all to make an offering of our bodies to God as "living sacrifices" which are "holy and pleasing to God." When we do this, we are offering him our "spiritual worship" (v. 1). Paul paints two graphic word pictures in v. 2. He actually commands us to stop *conforming* to the pattern of the world and to be *transformed* by allowing our minds to be renewed. As Paul wrote these two words in the Greek language of his day, they carried a significance that we can also appreciate in English. The word for 'conform' *(suschematizesthe)* can be defined as 'following a pattern or blueprint,' as in our English words *schema* and *schematic*. He's probably referring to those who blindly or legalistically follow the blueprint they have learned from societal or religious values. In contrast, the Greek word *metamorphousthe* calls for a *transformation* ('metamorphosis') from within, regardless of outside forces.

Earlier in Romans, Paul addresses the emptiness of secular, atheistic societies (ch.1) as well as legalistic Judaism (chs. 2–4). Then, from ch. 5 on, he introduces the dynamic fulfillment of a life justified through faith in Christ. Indeed, what he seems to be suggesting here is that Christianity isn't just about doing what you want, what everybody else is doing or what some code of rules says, it's letting Christ change you from the *inside-out*. It's about thinking with a *renewed mind*—in other words, *a metamorphosis must take place*. Only then will we be able to find God's "pleasing and perfect will." The logical sequence of these two verses ("I plead with you, sacrifice yourselves, don't conform, be transformed from within") suggests that Paul is calling on everyone (Gentile or Jew, male or female) to offer themselves to God and allow their minds to be set free from societal morays or religious dogma, which probably includes what they had been taught about women.

If God created women with some sort of imperfection, or placed it there after the Fall (something that would disqualify them from ministry), then why would women still be disqualified (or less qualified) once their minds were renewed?

THESIS # 27

Once one's mind is spiritually renewed, every believer may potentially exercise any spiritual gift.

Just as each of us has one body with many members, and these members do not all have the same function, so in Christ we who are many form one body, and each member belongs to all the others.

(Romans 12:4–5)

Let's suppose you are a deeply committed Christian woman who has just graduated with a Master's degree in Theology. Over the past several years, your husband, other students and professors have applauded your ability to teach and preach. You desire to serve God in pulpit ministry, but your denomination discourages women from preaching or teaching adults and refuses to ordain women to any ministry. A few other churches say they could use you as "Director of Education" or "Director of Children's Ministries." Sadly, the only denomination that will ordain you to pulpit ministry does not share your theological stand on some significant issues. What will you do? Before you make your decision, I hope you finish reading this book and several others listed in the References section at the end of this book, but for now, let's see if the rest of Romans 12 has any advice for people in your position.

Verse 3 suggests that there is no room for any category of Christian to consider him or herself to be more important than others; rather, we are all to evaluate ourselves with "sober judgment." Verses 4 and 5 point out that all of us (male and female) are part of the body of Christ, and all belong to each other. Obviously, some parts of every body, whether male or female, are more important than other parts, but one cannot use these verses to prove that only males can fill important positions in the body of Christ.

In vv. 6–9 Paul gives the first of several lists of spiritual gifts in the Bible. Notice that v. 6 says, "We have different gifts, according to the *grace* given us." This common New Testament word, *grace* (or *charis* in Greek) is often defined as 'God's undeserved, or unmerited, favor' shown to each one of us. Nothing suggests that certain gifts are given only to men. If that were true, somewhere in the New Testament, you would expect Paul to say, "We have different gifts, according to the *gender* given us." And even though the male pronoun is used consistently throughout ("If a *man's* gift," etc.), Paul cannot possibly mean that spiritual gifts are given only to men. In fact, in this verse there is no Greek word used that can be translated 'man.' TNIV gives a more accurate picture: "If *your* gift is…" Rather, our gifting depends on God's grace alone, dispensed equally to men and women.

Verses 9–16 spell out many kinds of actions and attitudes that are expected of Christians. The passage never suggests that women are better at some and only men can do others. Instead, Paul seems to be strongly encouraging all kinds of ministry for all kinds of people who are devoted to each other in love (v. 10), living in harmony (v. 16) and living at peace with each other (v. 18).

THESIS # 28

Paul's praise of Phoebe and several other women in Romans 16 suggests that he fully accepts women as deacons, elders or apostles.

I commend to you our sister Phoebe, a servant of the church in Cenchrea. I ask you to receive her in the Lord in a way worthy of the saints and to give her any help she may need from you, for she has been a great help to many people, including me.

(Romans 16:1–2)

At first glance, the last chapter of Romans reads like a group of in-formal greetings sent by Paul and his friends to their friends at the various "house churches" that were starting up. But to people inves-tigating how involved women were in ministry at that time, this chap-ter is a richly significant "who's who" of female activity in the early church. Of the twenty-five names listed, eight are women. For in-stance, Paul addresses Priscilla as one of the "fellow-workers in Christ Jesus" (v. 3); Epenetus: "dear friend" (v. 5); Junias: "out-standing among the apostles" (v. 7); Tryphena and Tryphosa: "work hard in the Lord" (v. 12); Persis: "worked very hard in the Lord" (v. 12). There is no doubt that the early church was deeply dependent on the various ministries capably offered by women.

"Wait a minute!" says the traditionalist. "We have no problem with women being involved in the church. But none of these words prove that they were permitted to be deacons or elders or do the preaching and teaching." How, then, can we explain why Paul would use terms like "co-worker" and "apostle" if he felt women should not be in those positions? Bilezikian points out that Paul's usage of the term "co-worker" often referred to church planters or "front-line pioneer missionaries" and "apostle" indicated "the highest level of leadership authority in the early church" (198). In John Bristow's book, *What Paul Really Said about Women*, he quotes early Church Fa-ther John Chrysostom's commendation of Junia: "Oh how great is the devotion of this woman, that she should be counted worthy of the appellation of apostle" (57). See Thesis # 70.

Clearly, the most surprising part of Romans 16 is the first two verses, quoted at the top of this thesis. Paul uses two significant words in relation to this woman, Phoebe. In the NIV, they are translated 'ser-vant' and 'great help.' The TNIV substitutes *deacon* for 'servant' and *benefactor* for 'great help.' Other translations replace 'great help' with *minister, patron, succourer* or *office-holder*. By now, you've probably figured out that Paul might be saying something pretty significant here—

perhaps something difficult to translate, or even introducing a concept early translators could not embrace.

This is a good place to digress for a minute and recommend a journal that I have subscribed to for years, called *Priscilla Papers*, the quarterly publication of an international organization I've already mentioned in this book: Christians for Biblical Equality. Their twentieth anniversary edition (autumn, 2006) is a "must have" collection of twelve scholarly articles by various authors. The one written by Mark Reasoner on Romans 16 is well researched, but also easy to read, and it will show you why this chapter (particularly these two verses) sheds so much light on gender equality in the churches in Paul's day. Reasoner raises a simple but often overlooked point: why would Paul spend forty words at the beginning of his final greetings to commend this woman named Phoebe (14)?

Paul chooses two specific Greek words to describe Phoebe. The first is *diakonon*, a fairly common word translated 'minister' eighteen times and 'deacon' three times in the King James Version, but translated 'servant' here when relating to Phoebe. I would expect that if Paul had been talking about a man in v. 1, seventeenth century translators would have used 'deacon,' but would never have associated this office with a woman. Sadly, many modern translations still use 'servant'; TNIV uses 'deacon.'

However, it might even be more remarkable that Paul describes Phoebe as a *prostates pollon*, which, addressed to a man, would probably be translated 'ruler of many.' The verb form (*proistemi*) occurs eight times in the New Testament and is usually connected to governing or ruling. For instance, in Romans 12:8 Paul states that if one's gift is "*leadership*, let him *govern*," and he recommends double honor for those elders "who *direct* the affairs of the church well" (1 Timothy 5:17, emphasis mine).

It was probably Phoebe who delivered the letter Paul wrote to the churches in Rome. If she was as competent a leader, deacon or elder as the verses suggest, she may even have stayed on in some of these churches to present, teach and amplify some of Paul's epistles. Under those circumstances, it would make perfect sense for Paul to ask the churches to "receive her in the Lord in a way worthy of the saints" and to admit that "she has been a great help to many people, *including me*" (emphasis mine). How refreshing if all of our churches welcomed gifted, competent female leadership in this fashion.

THESIS # 29

If God chooses foolish, lowly and despised men for ministry, why can he not choose women?

Brothers, think of what you were when you were called. Not many of you were wise by human standards; not many were influential; not many were of noble birth. But God chose the foolish things of the world to shame the wise; God chose the weak things of the world to shame the strong. He chose the lowly things of this world and the despised things . . . It is because of him that you are in Christ Jesus, who has become for us wisdom from God—that is, our righteousness, holiness and redemption.

(1 Corinthians 1:26–31)

Years ago, while reading *Women, Authority and the Bible*, edited by Alvera Mickelsen, I vividly recall being moved to tears when I read Gretchen Gabelein Hull's personal struggle in response to God's call upon her life. I hope you will identify with her pain as you read the following excerpt.

How many people are aware of the intense inner struggle a woman goes through after her spirit has been touched at a meeting or through a Bible passage, and she receives a call to ministry, only to be told, "You can't serve in that capacity because you are a woman"? There is guilt because she has repressed her call. There is frustration, even anger, with those who have denied her call. There is deep sorrow at being considered forever barred from answering that call (23).

How does God decide who to choose and call to Christian ministry? Corinth would never have been described as the seat of knowledge, nobility or wealth—and that's putting it mildly! But Paul begins the letter by thanking God for the fact that "in him you have been enriched in every way—in all your speaking and in all your knowledge" (1:4–5). Because Christ was "confirmed" in them (v. 6), Paul proclaims, "Therefore you do not lack any spiritual gift" (v. 7).

With that solid foundation set down, Paul describes what God thinks of the "worldly" wisdom of the wise man, scholar or philosopher—it will be destroyed (vv. 19–20). He explains how the Greeks of his day sought wisdom, whereas the Jews wanted miraculous signs, etc. The turning point is v. 24: *"But to those whom God has called…"* There's the difference! From vv. 24 to 28, Paul uses the word "call" twice and the word "choose" three times. You can almost hear him shouting, "I don't care about genealogy, intelligence or wealth. I just need to know one thing: *have you been called?* If you have, it's only because of Christ Jesus, who has become all the God-given wisdom anyone ever needs—our righteousness, holiness and redemption."

Craig Keener has written a very helpful book called *Paul, Women and Wives*. Regarding God's call to ministry, Keener explores the basis on which any *man* can prove his call, saying, "We [men] trust inner conviction and the fruit of holy lives and teaching and faithfulness to that call, and if these evidences are insufficient demonstration of divine calling in the case of our sisters, how shall we attest our own?" (120).

THESIS # 30

God's washing, sanctification and justification must fully redeem and equally equip every Christian woman or man, regardless of their past.

And that is what some of you were. But you were washed, you were sanctified, you were justified in the name of the Lord Jesus Christ and by the Spirit of our God.

(1 Corinthians 6:11)

If you're not quite sure what God considers sinful behavior, you might want to look up 1 Corinthians 6:9–10, where Paul lists a peculiar mixture of actions ranging from bad to worse. In God's eyes, anyone who continues to practice these things as a lifestyle is called "wicked." Although it is still possible for Christians to commit such actions on occasion, it is never God's intention. The moment we invite Christ to enter and rule our lives, three crucially important theological transactions take place: washing, sanctification and redemption. First, when we yield our lives to Christ, he promises he will spiritually reside in us. But before he takes up residence, Scripture tells us that he washes, or cleanses, us. It's as if God runs us through a spiritual car-wash and announces, "From this moment on, I declare that you are delivered from past dirt." Secondly, he "sanctifies" us. This concept has two meanings: he sets us apart from the rest of the world, but also declares us to be "holy" because of Christ's holiness in us. Lastly, Paul mentions that we are "justified," or declared to be righteous. So, Paul's three obvious points are: (a) we could not possibly wash our past actions or thoughts away; (b) we'll never make ourselves holy; and (c) no matter how good our actions are, we will never be declared righteous because of them. All of these theological declarations happen "in the name of the Lord Jesus Christ and by the Spirit of our God" (v. 11).

Why is all this important to the central topic of this book? If God can take any man who was a practicing idolater, adulterer, thief, slanderer or any other sleazy scum-bag, and clean him up—yes, even ordain him to positions of church leadership—why can (or will) he not do the same for any woman? God only has one spiritual car-wash: "the blood of Jesus, [God's] Son, purifies us [all] from all sin" (1 John 1:7).

THESIS # 31

Paul's advice to married couples regarding sexual fulfillment is completely gender-equal.

The wife's body does not belong to her alone but also to her husband. In the same way, the husband's body does not belong to him alone but also to his wife.

(1 Corinthians 7:4)

The seventh chapter of Paul's first letter to the Christians at Corinth is full of some pretty straightforward talk about marriage, sex and divorce, as you will see in this thesis statement and the next. The problem is, many things he says can be interpreted in more than one way. Take v. 1, for instance: "Now for matters you wrote about: It is good for a man not to marry." It sounds like a theme verse for a monastery! No doubt many a Catholic priest or single celibate has been encouraged by this verse on occasion. But the chapter goes on to show that Paul thinks marriage is a wonderful institution, and he gives advice on how to make it even better. Several scholars have suggested that what may be happening here is that the Corinthian Christians—many of whom practiced celibacy—had written to Paul to see what his opinion was. It might have gone something like this: "Now, about what you Corinthians suggested in your letter to me, 'It's good for a man not to marry,' let me tell you what I think. With all this sexual immorality around, it's better to have a wife or husband." Whatever the context really was may be lost in antiquity; nevertheless, Paul then launches into some great advice for any married couple. Notice the equality of the man and woman as he describes how the sexual aspect of marriage should work:

v. 2 "Each man should have his own wife, and each woman her own husband." (Equality, but the husband's desire is mentioned first.)

47

v. 3 "The husband should fulfill his marital duty to his wife, *and likewise* the wife to her husband." (Equality, but the wife's desire is mentioned first.)

v. 4 "The wife's body does not belong to her alone but also to her husband. *In the same way,* the husband's body does not belong to him alone but also to his wife." (Equality but the husband's desire is mentioned first.)

v. 5 "Do not deprive each other except by mutual consent..." (Neither is first.)

v. 5 "Come together again..." (neither is first).

In my private practice as a marriage counselor, I've had more than one woman complain that her church-going Christian husband demands that she meet his sexual needs based on the first half of v. 4 (The wife's body does not belong to her alone but also to her husband). Perhaps her husband—and a lot of other husbands—should humbly read all these verses (not just his favorite parts) with an open mind before going to bed! Seriously, how can anyone read anything into these verses other than complete equality between male and female sexual partners?

Paul also discusses the matter of frequency of sexual pleasure in v. 5. The ideal seems to be to not deprive each other unless it is by "mutual consent" and for an agreed-upon time, whereupon the couple should "come together again" lest Satan capitalizes on either one's weakness, prodding him/her to look for greener grass. Obviously, this does not imply that the absence of sexual pleasure ever justifies a greener grass impulse; rather, it suggests the need for an honest, ongoing and reciprocal discussion of the couple's desires. The coming together again paints a beautiful picture in the Greek language. Paul uses the word *symphonou,* from where we get our word "symphony." The implication is subtle: neither wife nor husband chooses the songs or conducts the orchestra, their only task is to lov-ingly ensure that their partner enjoys the music.

THESIS # 32

No one can be denied involvement in public ministry on the basis of rituals, gender or marital or social status.

I am saying this for your own good, not to restrict you, but that you may live in a right way in undivided devotion to the Lord.

(1 Corinthians 7:35)

There is hardly a chapter in the Bible that covers as many controver-sial issues as 1 Corinthians 7. Included in the list are the pros and cons of circumcision, slavery vs. freedom, celibate marriages, single-ness, divorce, separation and remarriage. No wonder various Chris-tians and church denominations differ widely over what Paul might have meant. But one fact cannot be disputed: Paul was obviously at-tempting to guarantee complete gender equality in these verses. You will appreciate the uniqueness of this intentional literary style even more if you read along in your own Bible. Notice the carefully ar-ranged male-female parallels in the following verses.

vv. 10–11: "A *wife* must not separate from her husband…a *hus-band* must not divorce his wife."

vv. 12–13: "If any *brother* has a wife who is not a believer and she is willing to live with him, he must not divorce her. And if a *woman* has a husband who is not a believer and he is willing to live with her, she must not divorce him."

v. 14: "For the unbelieving *husband* has been sanctified through his wife, and the unbelieving *wife* has been sanctified through her believing husband…"

v. 15: "But if an unbeliever leaves, let him do so. A believing *man* or *woman* is not bound in such circumstances."

v. 16: "How do you know, *wife,* whether you will save your husband? Or how do you know, *husband,* whether you will save your wife?"

vv. 32–34: "An unmarried *man* is concerned about the Lord's affairs….An unmarried *woman* or virgin is concerned about the Lord's affairs…"

vv. 32–34: "But a married *man* is concerned about the affairs of this world—how he can please his wife…But a married *woman* is concerned about the affairs of this world—how she can please her husband."

In these verses, Paul very carefully spells out the equal privileges and responsibilities that both men and women have in husband-wife relationships. There is no hint of male authority or dominance. Both are obligated to stay in the marriage if the other partner wants them to. Neither of them should divorce the other; yet, neither is bound to go after the one who leaves. Finally, both partners share a concern for the affairs of the world and a desire to please their spouse.

Although Paul obviously writes this passage to give advice about marriage, he purposely slips in two other controversial topics in the early church: circumcision and slavery (vv. 17–24). He doesn't mention these just to teach us about them (he does plenty of that elsewhere in his writings), but to compare them to various marriage scenarios. Three times, Paul tells the Corinthian Christians to stay in the situation they were in when God called them (vv. 17, 20 and 24). He also reminds them that God has called Christians to "live in peace" (v. 15). He's not saying these things to "restrict" them, but rather, that they *"live in a right way in undivided devotion to the Lord"* (v. 35). These points don't only apply to male and female situations, but also to slave or free, Jew or Gentile.

Now, you have every right to disagree with me, but I think verses 32–35 are what it's all about. Suppose you genuinely want to serve God and fully exercise any spiritual gift he has given you, but there are some incidents in your past that make you question your worthiness to minister. You have confessed these things to God, but you or others still keep dragging them up. After all these years, you still sort of see yourself as "damaged goods." I think this passage sets you free to be all you thought God wanted you to be when he called you. Were you circumcised or not circumcised? God doesn't care. Were you a slave (to anything) when God called you? He doesn't care, as long as you are now a slave only to him. Have you been separated, divorced or remarried? God doesn't care. Did you enter this world as a baby girl? God doesn't care. He *really doesn't care!* For every Christian man or woman, God only cares about two things: are you living in peace now, and are you living "in a right way in undivided devotion to the Lord" (v. 35)?

As we leave this thesis, objectively try to answer the following question. Which would upset God more: a male pastor/leader who is *not* living in a right way and is not devoted to his Lord, or a woman pastor/leader who *is* living in a right way in undivided devotion to her Lord?" While you're at it, you might want to compare this to Theses # 51 and # 64.

THESIS # 33

The traditional "chain-of-command" view of male headship can be interpreted to defend full gender equality and interdependency.

In the Lord, however, woman is not independent of man, nor is man independent of woman.

(1 Corinthians 11:11)

Early in this eleventh chapter of 1 Corinthians we read: "Now I want you to realize that the head of every man is Christ, and the head of the woman is man, and the head of Christ is God" (v. 3). For nearly two thousand years, verses such as this and Ephesians 5:22 have led most denominations to preach that God's divine plan is for men to be "head of the house" just as Christ is the head of man and God is the head of Christ. Apparently, the only party that is not the head of anyone or anything is woman. Various authors point out that the word "head" (Greek *kephale*) in 1 Corinthians 11:4 and 7 seems to have different shades of meaning than in v. 3.

This topic comes up again in Thesis # 60. For now, let's just note that the next few verses state that if a woman prays or prophesies with her head uncovered, she "dishonors her head" (probably meaning her husband—v. 4); yet, a man ought not to cover his own head (v. 7)—an action that supposedly would dishonor his "head" (Christ). The point to notice here is that a woman is allowed to prophesy and/or teach in church meetings, but she must meet the proper protocol of the day: that is, wear a head covering as a "sign of *authority* (Greek *exousian*) on her head, publicly signifying her equal right to participate in the service (v. 10).

Some authors make much of the phrase "the head of Christ is God," even suggesting that Christ's subservience to his Father is the divine model for wives' roles to husbands. In *Recovering Biblical Manhood and Womanhnood*, Wayne Grudem says, "We frankly recognize an eternal subordination of Christ to the Father," although he limits this subordination to "order and operation, not essence" (p. 457). Egalitarians staunchly reject this interpretation, and will only agree to Christ's *temporal* (not eternal) and voluntary subordination during his earthly ministry. They argue that all three persons of the Godhead must be equal in every way, citing the centuries-old Athanasian Creed to settle the argument: "…and in this trinity, there is no before or after; no greater or less, but all three persons are co-eternal together; and co-equal…worshipped in unity and the unity in trinity."

Australian author Kevin Giles has provided an outstanding defense for Christ's equality with the Father in his book, *The Trinity and Subordinationism*, in which he suggests that some current hierarchical authors may be in danger of redefining the Trinity to match or entrench their views of male-female relationships, stating that the growing trend to read subordination into the Trinity "has arisen exclusively in the context of arguing for the permanent subordination of women" (p. 115).

This passage is probably also responsible for women's hair usually being longer than men's, even in present society, and is undoubtedly why women have historically worn a hat or prayer covering in church (a practice still followed by some groups). In any event, the reason for all this seems to be given in vv. 8–9: *"For man did not come from woman, but woman from man; neither was man created for woman, but woman for man."*

If, indeed, the above verse is the biblical basis for an eternal, unchangeable truth, then most of us are in big trouble. You hardly ever see a hat on a woman in church anymore (well, maybe on Easter Sunday), and often women's hair is shorter than some men's. Sometimes we even see guys wearing baseball caps in church! So, did Paul really expect every society to follow these injunctions? For that matter, is he even directing the Corinthians to practice headship or male dominance at all? If he is, then explain the apparent contradiction of verses 11–12, where he says, *"In the Lord, however*, woman is not independent of man, nor is man independent of woman" (emphasis mine). The topic continues over the next two theses.

One way of reconciling this dilemma is to consider that vv. 2–10 may not even be Paul's words! Perhaps he is merely stating the Corinthian church's view (as he did in 7:1: "Now for matters *you* wrote about: 'It is good for a man not to marry.'" ref. Thesis # 31). In other words, Paul may be reiterating their position—even agreeing that it has a biblical base (v. 8)—but reminding them that there is another side to the argument as well. Yes, woman came from man. Valid point, Corinthians, but it's also true that every man since has been born by a woman. *The one cancels out the other!*

THESIS # 34

On at least one occasion, Paul seems to purposely introduce the definite article to reinforce his position on gender equality.

For as woman came from man, so also man is born of woman.

(1 Corinthians 11:12)

The point I'm now bringing up is fairly controversial. Find 1 Corinthians 11 and read v. 8: "For man did not come from woman, but woman from man." Now compare v. 9: "…neither was man created for woman, but woman for man." Notice that the NIV and TNIV do not use any definite articles (*the* man, *the* woman, etc.). Neither does the *New King James* version. In fact, most of the newer translations omit the articles throughout the passage.

What makes this passage interesting is this: in New Testament Greek, the definite article (usually translated 'the') is used quite randomly. Sometimes it precedes a noun, sometimes it does not. However, for some reason, Paul seems to deliberately use the Greek word for 'the' before each of the four nouns in v. 12, something he does not consistently do in vv. 4–11. Although most modern English versions (including the NIV and the TNIV) have left these occurrences of the definite article out, ironically, the old King James Version inserted all four of them: "as *the* woman is of *the* man, even so is *the* man also by *the* woman." One might assume that if Paul had deliberately meant women or men in general, he would have used no article. Or, if he had meant any man or any woman, he would have used the *indefinite* article (*a* man, *a* woman). His usage of "*the* woman" and "*the* man," repeated twice, leads some to speculate that there might be something far more significant here than meets the eye.

One must be careful not to read too much into this apparent enigma, but consider the possibility that Paul might be comparing the role of Adam to that of Jesus and the role of Eve to that of Mary. "For as *the* woman (Eve) came from *the* man (Adam), so also *the* man (Jesus) is born of *the* woman (Mary). Whatever sin's destructive devastation brought to male-female relationships, all is forgiven and forgotten through Christ's redemption.

THESIS # 35

The Holy Spirit alone determines which gifts or ministries to give to each person, regardless of gender.

Now to each one the manifestation of the Spirit is given for the common good. . . . All these are the work of one and the same Spirit, and he gives them to each one, just as he determines.

(1 Corinthians 12:7, 11)

Notice how Paul starts chapter 12: "Now about spiritual gifts, brothers, I do not want you to be ignorant" (v. 1) The word 'ignorant' basically means 'without knowledge.' Reading this passage through my faintly colored glasses, I just cannot see how anyone could arrive at anything but complete gender equality when it comes to the Holy Spirit's distribution of gifts. Verses 4 and 5 indicate that the Spirit gives Christians different kinds of gifts, service and work (for simplicity, think of them all as "spiritual gifts"), but there is absolutely no indication that women get one kind and men get another. Verse 6 could be confusing to some, as several translations read, "…the same God works all of them in all *men*," but TNIV more accurately translates "men" as "people." Verses 8–10 mention nine different gifts (wisdom, faith, prophecy, etc.), any one of which may be evident in any Christian. Verse 11 makes it abundantly clear: "All these are the work of one and the same Spirit, and he gives them to each one, just as he determines." As Gordon Fee concludes, "…God explicitly announced that he would pour out his Spirit on *all* people for prophetic ministry (Joel 2:28–29) where 'all' is explicitly defined in categories of men/women, slave/free and young/old" (254).

THESIS # 36

No member of the body of Christ is gender-specific or restricted from receiving the "greater gifts."

The body is a unit, though it is made up of many parts; and though all its parts are many, they form one body. So it is with Christ. For we were all baptized by one Spirit into one body—whether Jews or Greeks, slave or free—and we were all given the one Spirit to drink.

(1 Corinthians 12:12–13)

1 Corinthians 12 is one of the most straightforward passages in the Bible relating to what ministries women can do. Paul's description of how a physical body functions becomes a clear analogy of how the Holy Spirit functions in the church. Beginning at v. 24, he suggests that there is no priority or jealousy among our physical body parts (hands don't long to become ears and ears don't envy eyes, etc.). Instead, "God has arranged the parts in the body, every one of them, just as he wanted them to be" (v. 18). Verses 21–25 point out that no one part can say to another, "I don't need you!" because those parts that *seem* to be weaker are "indispensable." Rather, God gives even greater honor "to the parts that lacked honor, *so that there should be no division in the body.*" Paul's final observation about our physical body is v. 26: "If one part suffers, every part suffers with it; if one part is honored, every part rejoices with it."

Now for the application: "You are the body of Christ, and each one of you is a part of it" (v. 27). Paul then gives us what seems to be a prioritized list of spiritual gifts, somewhat parallel to the greater body parts: first apostles, then prophets, followed by teachers. The rest may be random. The issue is that many people do not think God would allocate these "greater gifts" to women. Yet, in Romans 12, Paul refers to Junias as "outstanding among the apostles," and Phoebe is probably seen as a deacon or elder (see Thesis # 27). For proof of women prophesying, check out Philip the Evangelist's daughters (Acts 21:9).

Some conclusions:

1. There is nothing in this passage that would restrict women from receiving any above-mentioned spiritual gift. And if the Spirit is going to give those gifts to women, surely he would expect women to use them.

2. There is no suggestion that the body's weaker or less honorable parts represent women any more than men. Both male and female bodies have a vast variety of parts, and together, they make up one unified body.

3. As our physical body gives greater honor to its "weaker" parts, so we must treat lesser giftedness with extra recognition and encouragement, whether found in men or women.

4. Just as there should be no division in the physical body, so we must ensure that we no longer divide the giftedness of our congregations along gender lines.

5. As with the physical body, if over half of our spiritual "body parts" continue to suffer (there are more women in churches than men) it behooves the rest of us to suffer with them (v. 26).

In his book, *Women in the Church,* Stanley Grenz makes this painful but accurate observation: "Nothing but jealousy, prejudice, bigotry and a stingy love of bossing in men have prevented woman's public recognition by the church. No church acquainted with the Holy Ghost will object to the public ministry of women" (54).

THESIS # 37

The examples of "agape love" in 1 Corinthians 13 are often more apparent in women than in men.

Love is patient, love is kind. It does not envy, it does not boast, it is not proud. It is not rude, it is not self-seeking, it is not easily angered, it keeps no record of wrongs. Love does not delight in evil but rejoices with the truth. It always protects, always trusts, always hopes, always perseveres.

(1 Corinthians 13:4–7)

Why have churches traditionally chosen men to be on the Leadership Board or Council of Elders? Why do many churches permit only men to receive and count the offering? Why are the communion elements usually prepared by women, but administered by men? Is it not because some of us have a predetermined stereotype in our minds that defines certain male and female roles? Important church decisions seem to require the objective, hard-nosed gifting that God has given to men. Sensitivity, softness and compassion are not usually seen as admirable qualities in leaders who must make the tough decisions.

In light of that, how ironic it seems that Paul would position the content of what we know as the thirteenth chapter of 1 Corinthians between the twelfth and fourteenth (of course, there were no chapter divisions originally). In 1 Corinthians 12, Paul deliberately explains how the gifts of the Holy Spirit work. Then, in chapter 14, he returns to Spirit gifting and warns how it can be misused. In the middle of these vitally important chapters, Paul seems to suggest that there may be something of even greater importance than gifting: what he calls *love,* or, more precisely, *unconditional* love (*agape* in Greek).

Read the verses that introduce this thesis again (1 Corinthians 13:4–7). Are the attributes mentioned apparent in the chairman of your church board? The deacons or trustees who maintain the building or park the cars? The businessmen who launch the building program? Do you see these qualities in abundance in your church elders? Chances are, these virtues are just as prominent in that faithful grandmother who looks after the nursery or the single mom in charge of your "prayer chain." When it comes to leadership in churches, perhaps our priority should be candidates with the gentler virtues who also manifest objective leadership skills, as 14:1 suggests: "Follow the way of love *and* eagerly desire spiritual gifts." Imagine how different our churches (and homes) would be if all male or female leaders memorized and practiced these attributes.

THESIS # 38

The specific instructions Paul gives for exercising the gifts of prophecy and tongues show no indication of gender preference.

Follow the way of love and eagerly desire spiritual gifts, especially the gift of prophecy.

(1 Corinthians 14:1)

In 1 Corinthians 14, Paul carefully spells out both the blessings and difficulties that accompany the use of prophecy and tongues in a congregation. As the reader probably knows, some denominations encourage the use of these gifts, while others feel the gifts were primarily meant for use by the early church until the New Testament had been completed. It is not the intention of this little book to take sides on that debate. I simply want to point out that Paul's lengthy instructions on how these gifts are to be used give ample indication that he is speaking to both men and women.

Paul begins by encouraging the Corinthian congregation to "follow the way of love and eagerly desire spiritual gifts, especially the gift of prophecy" (v. 1). As mentioned in the previous thesis, the fragrance of *agape* (unconditional) love, as defined in 13:4–7, must precede and permeate the use of any spiritual gift. This verse also suggests that the gift of prophecy is a gift of higher rank than tongues, perhaps because prophecy brings strengthening, encouragement and comfort to the believers (14:3). Go back and notice how Paul begins v. 2: "For *anyone* who speaks in a tongue…" Apparently, any man or woman who has the gift is invited to use it.

Now notice vv. 7–8. Paul uses the flute, harp and trumpet as a "show and tell" for how gifts work: "If the trumpet does not sound a clear call, who will get ready for battle?" The implication is that Christian men and women are *instruments* through which God's gifts can more tangibly be understood and appreciated. God is the message, we are the messengers. So, if God could speak through an inanimate object like a trumpet (and he has), then why would he not be more likely to speak through a woman? Unlike musical instruments, God has blessed us with *minds* that we are to purposely engage when we prophesy, pray or sing (v. 15). And nothing here suggests that God prefers men's minds over women's.

THESIS # 39

The command for women to be silent in church is addressing the issue of proper decorum within that culture.

As in all the congregations of the saints, women should remain silent in the churches. They are not allowed to speak, but must be in submission, as the law says. …But everything should be done in a fitting and orderly manner.

(1 Corinthians 14:33–34, 40)

In my Bible, the heading the publishers have inserted before 14:26 says "Orderly Worship." It seems to me they've got it right. Paul's main concern here is not that women should never say a word in church, but that they not disrupt the service. For the most part, even my hierarchical friends agree with this interpretation, although some congregations continue to require complete silence from women in the service.

It helps to understand that early Christian church meetings were not highly organized, having no prescribed liturgy or photocopied order of service. Basically, anything could happen—and often did. That's why Paul called for order. All were to take turns, being considerate of others and knowing when to sit down and let others participate. But there was apparently an even greater problem with the women. Until this time, only the Jewish men congregated together for worship and instruction in the Torah. Women were not a part of this, and seldom received instruction beyond what their husbands would tell them. Consequently, it seems women began taking advantage of this new-found freedom and were disrupting the service with their constant questions, probably addressed to their husbands. That's why Paul asks them to wait until they get home to get answers, so that the service could carry on smoothly. The reference to them being in submission (v. 34) is probably not referring to submission to their husbands here, but to the teaching authority and the overall decorum of the meeting. Craig Keener sums it up: "The short range solution was that the women were to stop interrupting the service; the long range solution was that they were to learn the knowledge they had been lacking" (88).

THESIS # 40

Although Eve is often blamed for the fall, Scripture places equal, if not greater, blame on Adam.

For since death came through a man, the resurrection of the dead comes also through a man. For as in Adam all die, so in Christ all will be made alive.

(1 Corinthians 15:21–22)

We have already established the obvious truth that both Adam and Eve sinned, and both suffered the consequences of their sin (Thesis # 8). Along with the above verses, we should include Romans 5:12: "Therefore, just as sin entered the world through one man, and death through sin, and in this way death came to all men…" When I read such verses, I wonder how so many centuries of theologians could continue to blame Eve for causing Adam to sin and—worse yet—for being the primary cause of God's judgment and condemnation of the entire world.

What these verses are probably implying is that "mankind"—that is, both the male *adam* and the female *adam (see thesis # 1)* together—are responsible. In her book, *Woman, be Free*, Patricia Gundry has said it well: "It does not matter which child takes the first cookie, nor does it matter how imaginative their excuses….they both knew; they were created equal; they both sinned" (21).

THESIS # 41

God's anointing and seal of ownership is available to every believer.

Now it is God who makes both us and you stand firm in Christ. He anointed us, set his seal of ownership on us, and put his Spirit in our hearts as a deposit, guaranteeing what is to come.

(2 Corinthians 1:21–22)

Paul is writing these words to everyone who made up the church at Corinth. Remember, Corinth was a community that knew next to nothing about Christianity. If they worshiped anything, it was probably the sex-goddess, Aphrodite (the Romans called her Venus). The city had built an elaborate temple, where her 1,000 priestesses offered their "services" to any who wanted to "worship" with them. No doubt, some of these Christians had pretty undesirable backgrounds. To put it mildly, they weren't exactly the cream of the Christian crop. But it takes a group just like them to prove my point. Listen to what Paul says: "It is God who makes both us [mature apostles like Paul] and you [baby believers with a shady past] stand firm in Christ" (v. 19). You see, nothing within us will keep us (or Paul, Silas or Timothy, for that matter) "standing firm" except an amazing, forgiving, compassionate God who has given us everything we need.

Verse 22 says that he "sets his seal of ownership" on us, putting his Spirit in our hearts as a "deposit, guaranteeing what is to come." It's something like that engagement ring some of you placed on your lover's finger. Technically, she wasn't your wife yet, but to both of you she was now "fully qualified" in every way. Multiply that a hundred-fold and you begin to understand how God sees us. Every child of God is fully God's child; whether untrained Corinthian, Jewish scholar, physician, fisherman or former temple priestess, *God sees us all the same*—vessels that his Holy Spirit can fill with his spiritual gifts. Shady past, race or gender must have no bearing on God's limitless provisions for his children.

THESIS # 42

Competence to minister is not innate in men or women; it can only come from God.

Such confidence as this is ours through Christ before God. Not that we are competent in ourselves to claim anything for ourselves, but our competence comes from God. He has made us competent as ministers of a new covenant—not of the letter but of the Spirit; for the letter kills, but the Spirit gives life.

(2 Corinthians 3:4–6)

The reason Paul sounds confident in this passage is because of the excellent results of his and Timothy's ministry in Corinth. In order to assure them he is not bragging, though, he is quick to point out that God did it all (through them). Verse 5 doesn't leave much doubt, does it? "Not that we are competent in ourselves to claim anything for ourselves, but our competence comes from God." I expect Paul would be the first to proclaim loud and clear that there was nothing in his life that made him competent—not his Jewish heritage, not his dual citizenship, not his extensive education and certainly not his gender! Maleness does not guarantee competence any more than femaleness hinders it.

Paul's competence comes from the God who made him a competent minister of a new covenant. That's the issue here. Paul is no longer under the old covenant of the "letter of the Law," but under the new covenant of the Spirit. Of all people, Paul would know how restrictive Judaism was to public ministry for women; he would also know that the gifting of the Holy Spirit brought life to anyone who wished to minister.

THESIS # 43

Both men and women are "jars of clay" and can equally experience the "all-surpassing power" that comes from God.

But we have this treasure in jars of clay to show that this all-surpassing power is from God and not from us.

(2 Corinthians 4:7)

We will explore this concept more fully in Thesis # 83, but let's take a minute now to appreciate its meaning. From the previous verse, we learn that the treasure Paul speaks of is the light God has placed in our hearts "to give us the light of the knowledge of the glory of God in the face of Christ" (v. 6). How amazing is this! God wants us to see his glory "in the face of Christ." The unapproachable image of an Old Testament God is replaced with the intimate knowledge and radiance of a personal Christ-God. What seems even more unbelievable to Paul is that God has placed this light in *jars of clay*! The imagery brings you up short: God no longer reveals himself distantly through golden temple vessels and costly priestly garments—he takes up residence in common clay jars, jars with nothing to boast about. Why? "…to show that this all-surpassing power is from God and not from us." He doesn't need decorated, titled, degreed, ordained jars. He doesn't require just male jars or Jewish jars. *Any old jar will do*, filled with God's all-surpassing power.

THESIS # 44

Both women and men can become completely new creations in Christ and be appointed by God to be his ambassadors.

Therefore, if anyone is in Christ, he is a new creation; the old has gone, the new has come! . . . God was reconciling the world to himself in Christ, not counting men's sins against them. And he has committed to us the message of reconciliation. We are therefore Christ's ambassadors, as though God were making his appeal through us.

(2 Corinthians 5:17–20)

Did you ever wonder what it would be like to be an ambassador? Imagine the power and prestige you would have. Ambassadors are the highest-ranking diplomats one country can send to another and historically were regarded as personal representatives of the country's king, emperor or president. That's exactly the word that Paul uses here in defining the job description of every Christian.

Before God could send any human being out as his ambassador, however, he had to re-create us. Paul says, "Therefore, if anyone is in Christ, he is a new creation; the old has gone, the new has come!" (v. 17). When he says "the old," he is probably referring to what we all were as a result of Adam and Eve choosing to disobey God. The old religious system (the Law) could never take away our sin, but Christ's death did just that. He met God's perfect standard in our place, and now we can be "reconciled," or brought back into line with God. Once we receive this incredible gift of sins forgiven, it becomes our mandate to reconcile others to God.

It has often been stated that, once you invite Jesus Christ to reign in your life, the position of ambassador is not optional. We're all ambassadors. Automatically! The question is, are we good ones or bad ones? Wherever we go, whatever we do, people see our King and his eternal country through us. If it was left up to religious leaders, some might only choose the most dedicated, educated and ordained men to represent our King, but the fact remains that all children of God have been reconciled and appointed by their King to represent him in this foreign land.

Consider this: many of our congregations only fill their high-ranking positions with men—deacons, elders, pastors, etc.—and restrict women from these offices. To me, that still has a legalistic sound to it, as if we're still under Old Testament Law. Convince me that Joe Citizen would make a better ambassador for Christ than Jane Citizen. Every Christian woman is also a completely new creation, fully reconciled to God (no defects) and commissioned (ordained?) to be a life-long ambassador for the King of Kings. Maybe it's time we at least let her serve communion or preach now and then.

THESIS # 45

If God can minister through Paul in spite of his weaknesses, he must be able to do the same through women.

But he said to me, "My grace is sufficient for you, for my power is made perfect in weakness." Therefore I will boast all the more gladly about my weaknesses, so that Christ's power may rest on me. That is why, for Christ's sake, I delight in weaknesses, in insults, in hardships, in persecutions, in difficulties. For when I am weak, then I am strong.

(2 Corinthians 12:9–10)

Many churches have a consistent stereotype of what elders and pastors should look like: they need to be strong, mature Christians. One pastor friend told me, "We won't allow women to be elders in our church because they get too emotional and upset about the issues we elders have to face. We need tough but deeply spiritual men who've been through the trenches."

Such comments remind me of Bilezikian's very humorous but all too accurate musings on Genesis 3:16:

> One gets weary of reading about the alleged susceptibility of Eve because of the emotional, volatile, impressionable, irrational, temperamental, impulsive, compliant, fragile, and passive psychological makeup of women; or that she was the likely candidate to

fall since women are incurably devious whereas men are honest, straightforward blokes (262).

If anybody has been through the trenches, it's the Apostle Paul (read 2 Corinthians 11:25–30), but I don't hear him telling us that elders and pastors have to be tough men who can take the heat. He's the first one to admit he sometimes gets depressed, even conceited, but he has learned the secret for any life or ministry: "My grace is sufficient for you, for my power is made perfect in weakness" (12:9). If it's weakness that God needs to demonstrate his power, then why wouldn't women also qualify?

THESIS # 46

Any privileged or disdained category caused by race, religion, status or gender is nullified by Christ's redemption.

You are all sons of God through faith in Christ Jesus, for all of you who were baptized into Christ have clothed yourselves with Christ. There is neither Jew nor Greek, slave nor free, male nor female, for you are all one in Christ Jesus.

(Galatians 3:26–28)

People like me, who feel strongly about women having the same opportunities as men in all types of ministry, probably emphasize Galatians 3:28 more than any other verse in the Bible. In fact, it's the theme verse for Christians for Biblical Equality—an organization that I have already brought to your attention in this book's introduction.

On the other hand, many deeply committed scholars look at these verses and feel that the first two categories (race, status) are quite different from the third (gender). Their thinking goes something like this: The position of elder or pastor is open to any Jew or Greek, slave or free (or any combination of those four) as long as that person is a man. But when Paul mentions women in the above verses, he is merely stating that in matters of salvation, Spirit-gifting and eternal life, women are in every way equal to men. However, they say the "role" of elder, teacher or pastor does not come from Spirit-gifting, but is a specific *office* that can only be held by men. Personally, I have trouble with that position. I'd like to think that if God meant the rules to be one way for *men* who were Jew/Greek, slave/free and another way for Jew/Greek, slave/free *women*, he could have helped Paul communicate it more clearly.

To illustrate, let's suppose your church is looking for a new pastor. You are the chair of the search committee, and only two applications have come in for the position. One is from a deeply spiritually committed woman—a seminary graduate, director of a large Christian organization and one who has shown abundant preaching and pastoral skills. The other is from an equally committed man who dropped out of school in the eleventh grade but later attended a Bible College for two years. Although he has never pastored a church, he feels strongly that God has commissioned him for this type of ministry. In this hypothetical situation, let's suppose you must decide between the two. Which would your church choose? Before you decide, consider Clarence Boomsma's opinion: "The equality of people's potential for worth, function, responsibility and authority lies in their unity with Christ, which is not restricted by their ethnicity, social status or gender" (39).

A further indication that women can now be full-fledged, card-carrying participants in any ministry might be what is revealed in v. 27: "For all of you who were *baptized* into Christ have clothed yourself with Christ." Something huge is taking place here. If God had wanted to continue the hierarchical practices of Jewish culture, the ritual of circumcision would have been continued—and, of course, it would be accessible only to males. By personal example, Christ replaces this with the gender-neutral practice of baptism.

THESIS # 47

Every Christian man and woman belongs to Abraham's spiritual seed and is therefore guaranteed all the benefits and inheritance of the firstborn male.

If you belong to Christ, then you are Abraham's seed, and heirs according to the promise. . . . when the time had fully come, God sent his Son, born of a woman, born under law, to redeem those under law, that we might receive the full rights of sons. . . . So, you are no longer a slave, but a son; and since you are a son, God has made you also an heir.

(excerpts from Galatians 3:29–4:7)

Let's go back a few verses to Galatians 3:26 and remind ourselves what Paul says to all the churches in Galatia: "*You are all sons of God.*" That's right; the Greek word is definitely 'sons.' Okay, it sounds as if he's just writing to the men in those churches, but 4:4 clears this up: God sent his Son to redeem (buy back) those who had lived by the legalism of the Old Testament, so that we (men and women) might receive the *full rights of sons!* You see, in Jewish families the firstborn son was the primary heir. If his parents died, he got the farm—not his sister, or even a younger brother. The firstborn son got the inheritance.

Jesus Christ completed his work of redemption. Nothing else needs to be done. Everyone gets the same inheritance as the oldest Jewish son would receive. Whatever Christ's death, burial and resurrection accomplished, it accomplished for every believer, regardless of race, social strata or gender. Compare this to Thesis # 88.

THESIS # 48

Of all the means a Creator-God could have chosen to give his Son a physical body, it seems supremely significant that he would choose a woman's womb.

God sent his Son, born of a woman…

(Galatians 4:4)

This is the third thesis point we have squeezed out of this section of Scripture—further proof of how significant this entire passage is to the topic. And most significant of all are the four words: "*born of a woman.*" Consider that a wife was little more than a chattel in many Jewish homes. Consider that a Jewish man could divorce his wife simply by saying "I divorce you!" three times. Consider how many Jewish men would pray, thanking God that they were not born a woman. Consider that generations of historians and theologians have berated women as being the cause of Adam's downfall. Consider how many churches still do not let women serve communion or teach an adult class. Consider all the above and much more. How do you account for God stepping in and hand-picking a teenage Jewish girl to incarnate his Son?

More than once, I've been moved by a statement Patricia Gundry made in *Women, Authority and the Bible*, edited by Alvera Mickelsen. It eloquently wraps up this thesis topic: "So many ironies of woman's conditioning hinge on her capacity to give birth. She presented the body and blood of the Savior to the world, yet she is prohibited from presenting the elements representing that body and blood at the Communion table" (17).

95 MORE FOR THE DOOR

THESIS # 49

Freedom in Christ that does not open all ministries to all believers is still a form of slavery.

It is for freedom that Christ has set us free. Stand firm, then, and do not let yourselves be burdened again by a yoke of slavery.

(Galatians 5:1)

This verse sounds a bit redundant, doesn't it? "It is for freedom that Christ set you free." The usual response would be, "Yes, I understand; Christ has set us free," but do we fully grasp why Christ has set us free? That's the crucial point he wants us to get—the whole purpose of Christ setting us free from the law is for us to purposely, undeservedly, deliriously keep on enjoying *complete freedom* in Christ. Because we are *free from* the Law, we are now *free to* worship and minister in ways the Law would not permit. This is why we must stand firm! The moment we relax our grip on it, the Law is right there, waiting to make us its slave all over again.

THESIS # 50

Paul replaces the Jewish rite of male circumcision with a gender-neutral requirement: faith expressed in love.

Mark my words!...You who are trying to be justified by law have been alienated from Christ; you have fallen away from grace. But by faith we eagerly await through the Spirit the righteousness for which we hope. For in Christ Jesus neither circumcision nor uncircumcision has any value. The only thing that counts is faith expressing itself through love.

(Galatians 5:2; 4–6)

72

Whenever you read someone as influential as Paul saying "Mark my words!" it's probably good to find out why he's saying it. A direct translation from Greek would be more like: "Behold! I, Paul, tell you!" So, why does he want us to "listen up"? It's all about Gentiles getting circumcised. He's saying that if you meaningfully choose to take part in that ritual, then you'd better be ready to adopt the rest of the Law as well; otherwise, you'll be a hypocrite. You can't be declared righteous just by observing a bunch of rules; all you end up doing is wandering away from the joyful freedom that grace brings.

The last part of verse 6 would be a good motto for churches to adopt in some of the sticky semi-legalistic practices that divide us: "The only thing that counts is faith expressing itself through love." One church lets a woman teach children; another insists she wear a hat; still another will permit her to preach as long as she isn't ordained; yet another allows equal opportunity in ministry, but insists on the wife's inequality to her husband. Wherever you end up on the legalistic ladder, the cold fact remains: you're still on the legalistic ladder.

THESIS # 51

The primary prerequisite for professional ministry is one's crucifixion to the world—an act required by both genders.

Not even those who are circumcised obey the law, yet they want you to be circumcised that they may boast about your flesh. May I never boast except in the cross of our Lord Jesus Christ, through which the world has been crucified to me, and I to the world. Neither circumcision nor uncircumcision means anything; what counts is a new creation.

(Galatians 6:13–15)

Once again, Paul is warning the early churches about the dangers of measuring one's internal maturity by the presence of external factors.

73

Basically, here's the point: getting circumcised won't make you any more qualified to minister. Besides, if circumcision approves men, then that means women can never be approved. For that matter, if maleness approves men, then we are simply making choices based on another external factor (maleness), or, at least, rejecting women because of the absence of that external factor. Sometimes I wonder whether or not we have allowed official titles (elder, deacon, pastor) to become external prerequisites, reserved for those with certain external attributes (like maleness). I find it interesting that the one factor Paul continues to boast about is not his race, formal training or maleness, but simply the Cross of our Lord Jesus Christ, through which a spiritual (internal) circumcision takes place for both men and women.

In the final analysis, all that counts is "a new creation" (v. 15). Paul tells the Corinthians the same thing: "If anyone is in Christ, he is a new creation; the old has gone, the new has come!" (2 Corinthians 5:17—Thesis # 44). That raises a very dicey question: do men receive a higher caliber of "new creation" at their conversion than do women? If both are truly, completely re-created spiritually at conversion, then on what basis can we withhold any ministry from women?

THESIS # 52

The God who destroyed the wall of hostility between Jews and Greeks can certainly destroy the "gender wall."

But now in Christ Jesus you who once were far away have been brought near through the blood of Christ. For he himself is our peace, who has made the two one and has destroyed the barrier, the dividing wall of hostility, by abolishing in his flesh the law with its commandments and regulations His purpose was to create in himself one new man out of the two, thus making peace, and in this one body to reconcile both of them to God through the cross…Consequently, you are no longer foreigners and aliens, but fellow citizens with God's people and members of God's household…

(Ephesians 2:13–16, 19)

The sacrificial work of Christ's crucifixion and resurrection met the needs of all people, from the most derelict of Gentiles to the most devout Jew, thereby creating a new race. It wasn't that Gentiles simply had to become Jews. What good would it do for the ones farther away simply to move nearer? Neither of them qualified! Christ must create in himself "one new man" or, as in TNIV, "new humanity" out of the two (v. 15). What is the end result of all this? In God's household, there are no foreigners and aliens, only "fellow citizens with God's people and members of God's household"(v. 19).

I have raised this question before, but please ponder the significance of it once again: Given that the foulest Gentile man may fully and freely join God's household of believers and potentially become an elder, teacher or pastor, why, then, must deeply spiritual women doubt their call to certain ministries and be treated as aliens and foreigners in the same household?

THESIS # 53

Paul, the most revered of all missionary-apostles, says he is less worthy than all God's people— which must include women.

I became a servant of this gospel by the gift of God's grace given me through the working of his power. Although I am less than he least of all God's people, this grace was given me: to preach to the Gentiles the unsearchable riches of Christ…

(Ephesians 3:7–8)

Hardly any comment is necessary. Paul's apostleship is not bestowed on him by any man-made organization, but by the gift of God's grace. He sees himself as "the least of all God's people"—which supposedly includes women—yet, God's grace alone is what enables him to preach to the Gentiles. By now, you probably know what I'm going to ask: If God's grace alone qualifies Paul to preach, why can it not qualify anyone to preach?

THESIS # 54

Being filled to the measure of all the fullness of God is a privileged right and God's desire for every Christian man or woman.

And I pray that you, being rooted and established in love, may have power, together with all the saints, to grasp how wide and long and high and deep is the love of Christ, and to know this love that surpasses knowledge—that you may be filled to the measure of all the fullness of God. Now to him who is able to do immeasurably more than all we ask or imagine, according to his power that is at work within us, to him be glory in the church and in Christ Jesus throughout all generations, for ever and ever! Amen.

(Ephesians 3:17–21)

Prayerfully consider these observations: Paul's prayer is that Christians "may be filled to the measure of all the fullness of God" (v. 19). Can women be filled to the same measure as men can, or is Paul only speaking to men? If he is addressing men, why does he not say so? Can only men receive "immeasurably more" than all they ask or imagine? Does this mean it is wrong for a woman to imagine herself being an elder or pulpit teacher? Is God's power only immeasurable for men, but limited for women? The purpose of Paul's prayer is to bring glory to Christ and his church "throughout all generations, for ever and ever" (v. 21). Does this mean that certain ministries will be withheld from women forever? Can you give me a good reason why?

THESIS # 55

The distribution of spiritual gifts by God to the church shows no indication that they are for men only.

But to each one of us grace has been given as Christ apportioned it. . . . It was he who gave some to be apostles, some to be prophets, some to be evangelists, and some to be pastors and teachers…

(Ephesians 4:7, 11)

It is obvious that God's gift of grace (undeserved or unmerited favor) has been given to each and every Christian "as Christ apportioned it." In other words, God has freely decided who gets which gift or gifts. It clearly states that he "gave some to be" apostles, prophets, evangelists, pastors or teachers. Some churches restrict the exercise of most, if not all, of these gifts to men. But, for the life of me, I see no indication that this section of Ephesians is any different from the rest of the book, which is addressed "To the saints in Ephesus, the faithful in Christ Jesus" (1:1). If some of these gifts were meant to be apportioned to men only, why didn't Paul say so? He could easily have started v. 11 of chapter 4 by saying, "Women, let me direct a few thoughts to the men in the church…" That would have cleared up everything. But he plainly sets down the rules for gifting: (a) God's grace is distributed by Christ however he decides, (b) some of us purposely get certain gifts and others purposely get other gifts, and (c) gender has nothing to do with it.

THESIS # 56

The purpose of God giving gifts to his followers is to move them all toward greater maturity in faith and knowledge.

...to prepare God's people for works of service, so that the body of Christ may be built up until we all reach unity in the faith and in the knowledge of the Son of God and become mature, attaining to the whole measure of the fullness of Christ.

(Ephesians 4:12–13)

Notice the sequence here. The purpose of God giving gifts to Christians is clear: to prepare every man and woman in his church to do "works of service." The purpose of these works of service is clear: to help build and grow the body of Christ. The purpose of that growing process is clear: to bring unity of faith and knowledge of Christ as everyone strives to reach the "whole measure of the fullness of Christ" (v. 13).

I enjoy attending annual conferences or conventions where all the local churches appoint delegates to conduct the business of the denomination. Eagerly, I look over the brochure to see which of the excellent workshops or seminars I'll sign up for. Maybe I'll catch up on some new theological trend or the latest pastoral counseling program, complete with big glossy binder and free CDs. Right about then, I read that the ministerial association (and other men) are invited for dinner to hear a famous Bible expositor, while the "wives" have their own banquet to hear how they can "Be All You Can Be and More—With Make-up Tips You Can Afford—on a Pastor's Salary" or something just as deep. My wife, a hospital chaplain, breaks protocol and sneaks in with me. No one has complained about her make-up yet.

In the average evangelical church today, over half of the attendees are women, many of whom are not given equal opportunity to mature biblically and theologically. Between teaching children's classes and serving in junior church or nursery during the morning message, getting the "goodies" ready for coffee after the service, or keeping their own children quiet during the service while their husbands take detailed notes, the myth of gender inequality is perpetuated.

The uneducated and unqualified female majority of God's family is restricted to certain acceptable "works of service," thereby providing little or no opportunity for women to be "built up" and mature in their knowledge and "measure of the fullness of Christ." Too often this sad sequence disqualifies them from ministry in the supposedly more significant "works of service" reserved for the male minority.

THESIS # 57

Every member of the body of Christ is encouraged to grow and "build itself up in love as each part does its work."

Then we will no longer be infants, tossed back and forth by the waves, and blown here and there by every wind of teaching and by the cunning and craftiness of men in their deceitful scheming. Instead, speaking the truth in love, we will in all things grow up into him who is the Head, that is, Christ. From him the whole body, joined and held together by every supporting ligament, grows and builds itself up in love, as each part does its work.

(Ephesians 4:14–16)

Men are every bit as vulnerable to false teaching and "cunning craftiness" as women are. The situation in most early churches was that the Jewish men had received years of teaching, but it was all new to the women. Consequently, women were prime targets for any false cult or philosophy that was making the rounds. Ironically, today's situation is not that different, if you consider the steady stream of self-help television "gurus" that fill any stay-at-home parent's day. Without years of sound teaching behind them, all Christians—men or women—are vulnerable.

Paul emphasizes that the entire body needs to help hold each other together. A healthy church makes sure that "every supporting ligament" (gender-neutral, notice) must keep on growing and building itself up "as each part does its work." Tomorrow's effective church needs to be a well-taught, gifted and skilled group of men and women who will hold each other accountable for growth and truth and unselfishly applaud and encourage each developing gift, regardless of gender.

THESIS # 58

When congregations meet for worship or teaching, all spiritually mature women and men are encouraged to publicly participate.

Speak to one another with psalms, hymns and spiritual songs. Sing and make music in your heart to the Lord, always giving thanks to God the Father for everything, in the name of our Lord Jesus Christ.

(Ephesians 5:19–20)

Paul surely intends the above verses to describe how a worship service should be conducted. Anyone may begin spontaneously speaking, singing or giving thanks at any time. Of course, order and decorum are still required (1 Corinthians 14, Thesis # 39). As in other passages already discussed, nothing here would indicate the slightest gender difference. A stranger walking in would have no idea whether a man or woman was in charge.

THESIS # 59

In public worship, men and women are clearly directed to submit to each other.

Submit to one another out of reverence for Christ.

(Ephesians 5:21)

I single out this verse for a thesis statement of its own because it seems to be a pivotal point in Paul's instructions. We egalitarians would love to convince you that this statement belongs with the next paragraph—not the previous one—thereby suggesting wives' and husbands' equal submission to each other (see TNIV). The source of confusion is that the Greek verb *hypotasso* (to voluntarily place oneself under) occurs in v. 21 ("*Submit* to one another out of reverence for Christ"), but v. 22 does not actually contain any Greek verb and can literally be translated 'wives to your husbands' by sort of hitch-hiking on the verb in v. 21. Some English translations insert the verb 'submit' in v. 22 in an attempt to clarify what Paul meant, but it really doesn't clarify anything. And, because New Testament Greek used no paragraphs, we'll never know whether or not v. 21 was meant to address how churches should function and v. 22 how husbands and wives should function.

In all fairness, if the word 'submit' in v. 21 includes husbands submitting to wives, it is the only place in the Bible where *hypotasso* (submit) is used in this way; yet wives are exhorted to submit to husbands in several places. Hopefully, the one thing we can agree on is that, within the church service, men and women are to submit to each other out of reverence for the Christ they are worshiping. The next four thesis statements may shed further light on this difficult passage.

THESIS # 60

A wife's submission to her "head" is primarily to be understood as submission to the Lord.

Wives, submit to your husbands as to the Lord. For the husband is the head of the wife as Christ is the head of the church, his body, of which he is the Savior. Now as the church submits to Christ, so also wives should submit to their husbands.

(Ephesians 5:22–24)

Did you read the two verses above? Then, you just read probably the two most controversial verses in the Bible relating to male-female roles. Literally thousands of pages have been written on these verses.

If this is something you really want to study deeply, I suggest that you get acquainted with some of the following authors: Gilbert Bilezikian, Craig Keener, Walter Liefeld, Richard and Catherine Clark Kroeger, Alvera Mickelsen and Patricia Gundry, not to mention scores of other authors who have done serious research into this topic. All of the authors I named above interpret or apply this passage in a gender-equal way. Less has been written on the hierarchical side, simply because Scripture has usually been assumed to teach hierarchy throughout the years. However, the rapid proliferation of scholarly books teaching equality has created the need for traditionalists to publish articles and books to validate their position. As I mentioned in Thesis # 23, John Piper and Wayne Grudem have compiled and edited an exhaustive list of articles by various authors, titled, *Recovering Biblical Manhood and Womanhood* (1991). Although the egalitarian authors listed above don't agree with Piper and Grudem's traditional conclusions, any serious student should make a careful study of their book, along with others in that camp.

Much of the disagreement over these verses centers on the significance of the words "submit" and "head." As explained in the previous thesis, submission is something that can only be done voluntarily (hence, TNIV: "Wives, submit *yourselves*…"), similar to our voluntarily submission to our Lord. No one is making us do it. Some authors suggest that Jewish men probably repeated the "Submit to your husband" phrase harshly and frequently to their wives. Paul may be suggesting that, regardless what picture you had of submission before, from now on think of it as how you would voluntarily give yourself to Christ. Paul Jewett concludes, "The subordination of the woman, then, is primarily and essentially to the Lord…" (80).

That leaves the word 'head' to deal with. This Greek word *kephale* can mean 'boss' or 'source of origin.' By now, you've probably figured out that the hierarchy camp translates it 'boss' or 'someone in a position of authority over'. Tie these verses together with 1 Corinthians 11:3 (Thesis # 33) and you'll see how plausible this "chain of command" sounds: God is the head of Christ, Christ is the head of husbands, husbands are the head of wives, wives are the head of no one. On the other hand, if 'head' means 'source', or 'priority of origin', Paul may simply be saying that woman (Eve) found her source in Adam, as Christ finds his (eternal) source in God. What matters is that we all find our source in Christ. Frankly, the two camps have gone back and forth on this one for years, and will continue to do so. Alan F. Johnson has written a great article exploring all of this in the Fall 2006 edition of *Priscilla Papers* (21).

I can't prove this, but I kind of wonder if Paul isn't taking what might have been a legalistic, male-dominant Jewish/secular rant, "Wives, submit to your husbands!" (a line that wives were thoroughly sick of hearing) and reminding Christian husbands that Christ willingly, sacrificially chose to *love*, not *rule* his bride (the church). From now on, wives are free from the Law (so are slaves, by the way, if you reference 1 Peter 2:18), free to view submission in a whole new light they've never seen before—a personal, voluntary choice. Some of today's cognitive psychologists refer to this as *reframing* (also *reformulation* or *labeling* (Gilliland, James & Bowman, p. 246), a technique which, according to Sheldon Rose, "attempts to change the point of reference against which the clients judge their behaviors and cognitions" (211). It's like that old family portrait that has hung on your wall for years. One day you happen to see it in a new light or from a different angle. Or maybe Uncle Louie explains who the guy in the back row *really* is. From that moment on, the picture takes on a new "point of reference" and will never be viewed the same.

THESIS # 61

Christ's act of giving himself up for the Church becomes the supreme example of how a husband should love his wife.

Husbands, love your wives, just as Christ loved the church and gave himself up for her to make her holy, cleansing her by the washing with water through the word...

(Ephesians 5:25–26)

What was Paul thinking when he wrote the above words? He had just made it clear that submission to each other in church meetings is necessary and explained that a woman's submission to her husband is, first and foremost, a voluntary submission to Christ the Lord. However, I'm sure he was also keenly aware of the uproar he might cause by even slightly suggesting that a Jewish man should submit to his wife. It may have been a stroke of genius on Paul's part (or Spirit-guidance) that caused him to choose the Greek verb *agapao* (love), not *hypotasso* (submit), to reach the male audience. Of the several Greek New Testament words that can be translated 'love,' only this one carries the concept of loving unconditionally, with no strings attached. It's the kind of love that keeps on loving just because you choose to love, even when no love is being returned. New Testament commentator A. S. Wood considers it to be "the highest and distinctively

Christian word for loving" (76). That's why the best known verse in the Bible (John 3:16) tells us that God *unconditionally loved* the world so much that he gave us his one and only Son to die in our place.

I doubt if husbands anywhere in the world, Jew or Gentile, had ever before been told to love their wives in this way. Even today's husbands would sit up and take notice: "You mean, I'm supposed to keep on loving my wife even when she shows no love to me?" Exactly. But wait, there's more. You are also supposed to *give yourself up* for her in the same way as Christ gave himself up for us. She needs to know that her well-being is more important to you than your own well-being. The reason for doing this is two-fold: she will then feel not only loved, but also holy and cleansed.

Are we responsible for our wives' holiness and cleansing? It does sound a bit far-fetched. Obviously, what Paul is actually talking about here is what Christ did for his church; it was only Christ who could make us holy in God's sight and cleanse us from our sin. But why would Paul bring that up when he's talking about how husbands should love their wives? I think Paul is reminding us that Christ's death, resurrection, etc. guaranteed that every child of God could now be declared holy and cleansed from sin. Men of Paul's day (Jewish or otherwise) continued to treat women as if they were less holy—not quite cleansed, and certainly not equal to their husbands. It must have been earth-shattering for these newly-converted Christian husbands to hear Paul tell them to unconditionally love and offer themselves up for their wives.

Now v. 25: "Husbands, love your wives, just as Christ loved the church and gave himself up for her." My experience as a Marriage and Family Therapist for the last three decades has shown me that there are a lot of husbands who believe that they are to love their wives in the same way as Christ will one day rule in the millennium (when Christ returns to earth to reign for a thousand years as King of Kings). No, the Christ Paul is referring to is the humble, broken, crucified Savior who loved the world more than he loved himself—a noble but attainable goal for any husband.

THESIS # 62

As Christ makes the Church radiant, so a husband's goal is to make his wife radiant.

...and to present her to himself as a radiant church, without stain or wrinkle or any other blemish, but holy and blameless.

(Ephesians 5:27)

At this point, Paul seems to purposely drop another "bombshell" word that probably got every man's attention in that day. The Greek word *doxa*, which is translated here as 'radiant'" can also mean 'glorious', 'dazzling', 'gorgeous', 'honored', 'sparkling' or even 'finely dressed' (all of these are used in the old KJV to translate *doxa*). Paul is simply saying, "Husbands, just as Christ did what was necessary to make his bride (church) feel fully cleansed, forgiven, honored, radiant and glorious, so we are to care for our wives—and churches are to care for their believing sisters.

You men who are spiritually mature and actively involved in your church —have you ever thought about how fortunate you are? God chooses to use even a man as human as you to be an elder or deacon. You have the right to sit on your church council or even preach now and then when the Pastor is away. Such a privilege should make your face beam with tears of gratitude. Undeserving as you are, Christ makes you part of his spotless bride, and as such, allows you to hold important leadership positions in his church.

Or you may be an ordained minister, like me. Just think what Christ, our bridegroom, has done for us! We, who could never deserve to be his bride, can go through every day of our lives with humble hearts and radiant faces because our God has made us holy and blameless. With all the wrinkles, blemishes and dark secrets of our past, we should have been disqualified from "ordained" ministry (a term, by the way, that is never found in Scripture). There's nothing about us that deserves to have people call us "Reverend." We, who deserve only condemnation from God, stand in his presence and his pulpits completely righteous and radiant through Christ. Whatever position or title has been bestowed on us, whether by our society or by our Savior, it must also extend to all washed and radiant women who are presently denied similar positions and titles. In the foreword to her book, *Neither Slave Nor Free,* Patricia Gundry has penned a timely reminder for us "Revs": "You must know that ordination, that sought after and longed for credentialing, is a totally human invention" (foreword, i).

Church leaders, may you nurture and commend (ordain) Spirit-gifted women to all levels of ministry. Congregations, may you reach new levels of radiance, purity and holiness as you ensure *all* your members, male and female, have equal benefits and opportunities. Christian husband, put a life-long smile on your wife's face as you give yourself up for her. And Christian woman, may you never again view yourself as unequal, unqualified, inadequate, less forgiven or less redeemed than any other part of the bride of Christ.

THESIS # 63

The bare minimum of a husband's love for his wife should be greater than the amount of love he shows himself.

In this same way, husbands ought to love their wives as their own bodies. He who loves his wife loves himself. After all, no one ever hated his own body, but he feeds and cares for it, just as Christ does the church—for we are members of his body.

(Ephesians 5:28–30)

Back in 1953, an American psychiatrist named Harry Stack Sullivan wrote: "When the satisfaction or security of another person becomes as significant to one as is one's own satisfaction or security, then the state of love exists" (43). Read that again. Husband, does this quotation describe how you show love to your wife? Could you honestly sign your name to that statement? If you could, then you're almost there.

"What do you mean, *almost* there?" I can imagine the anger and frustration on your face. Does God expect more than the above from any husband? Yes. We are supposed to love our wives "in this same way" as Christ loves every part of his bride: with consistent *agape* love (read Thesis # 61 again). Unconditional Christ-like love takes Sullivan's definition up a notch: "When the satisfaction or security of another person becomes *more* significant to one than is one's own satisfaction or security, then the state of *agape* love exists." Sullivan's words are well chosen: s*atisfaction* and *security*. The greatest thing Christ offers human beings is the constant assurance of their satisfaction and security—traits frequently deficient in women's (and men's) lives.

THESIS # 64

Paul prays that all Philippian believers would grow in knowledge, insight and discernment—attributes often assumed to be more evident in men.

And this is my prayer: that your love may abound more and more in knowledge and depth of insight, so that you may be able to discern what is best and may be pure and blameless until the day of Christ, filled with the fruit of righteousness that comes through Jesus Christ—to the glory and praise of God.

(Philippians 1:9–11)

Charles O. Knowles, in his book, *Let Her Be,* reports that in 1995, a certain seminary hosted the Clyde T. Francisco Preaching Awards. The all-male committee ranked audiotapes of 28 written sermons and chose the top three for the award. Knowles says, "To their surprise, and to the horror of the trustees…the voices were those of three women," who, according to Knowles, "now stand accused of violating scripture for preaching the pure word of God better than did the other 25 [male] contestants" (238).

This incident reminds me of the above verses, where Paul is praying for the entire church (men and women) at Philippi. Let's suppose your church was looking for a new pastor, and your board received a glowing letter of recommendation similar to this:

I can assure you that the candidate you are considering:

— *abounds more and more in knowledge and depth of insight*

— *is able to discern what is best*

— *will be pure and blameless until the day of Christ*

— *is filled with the fruit of righteousness*

— *is living life to the glory and praise of God*

What church wouldn't want to extend a call to this candidate immediately? But imagine their consternation when *she* arrives! There are countless exhortations throughout the Bible that we hold up as benchmarks for committed Christian ministry. When we see men who exemplify them, we send them off to seminary and ordain them. Yet, seminary-trained women of equal ilk who then seek pulpit positions seldom get their application past the church's paper shredder.

THESIS # 65

Paul is far more concerned that the gospel be preached than in the gender of the preacher.

It is true that some preach Christ out of envy and rivalry, but others out of good will. The latter do so in love, knowing that I am put here for the defense of the gospel. The former preach Christ out of selfish ambition, not sincerely, supposing that they can stir up trouble for me while I am in chains. But what does it matter? The important thing is that in every way, whether from false motives or true, Christ is preached. And because of this I rejoice.

(Philippians 1:15–18)

Aren't Paul's words above somewhat surprising? If an ordained minister in your denomination was continuing to preach out of envy, rivalry and selfish ambition without sincerity, one would hope that the denominational leaders would recall his ordination papers. Yet, Paul doesn't get uptight about these vagabond preachers. His take on the whole scene is this: Even if people's motives are false, even if they show envy and keep fighting with each other, Christ is being preached—and that's "the important thing" (v. 18). Obviously, Paul is not minimizing the need for pastors to be pure, devoted examples to their flock, but he's placing things in their proper perspective; people can learn about Christ even through a less-than-perfect vessel.

If Paul exhorts us to put up with unscrupulous male preachers, even if they are trying to "stir up trouble," one would think he may have left room for the occasional spiritually committed, well-trained woman to try her hand at the same task as well.

THESIS # 66

After a compelling call for unity and like-mindedness, Paul exhorts us to adopt the same attitude as that of Christ Jesus.

Your attitude should be the same as that of Christ Jesus: Who, being in very nature God, did not consider equality with God something to be grasped, but made himself nothing, taking the very nature of a servant, being made in human likeness. And being found in appearance as a man, he humbled himself…

(Philippians 2:5–8)

The church at Philippi must have been a superior group of Christians. Paul calls them "saints" (1:1) and mentions their "partnership in the gospel" (1:5) and their "progress and joy in the faith" (1:25). He seems overjoyed to be writing to them and is very upbeat as he encourages them to "be like-mined, having the same love" (2:2), and to humbly "consider others better than yourselves" (2:3)—all very gender-equal directives, by the way. Then, in 2:6 Paul paints a graphic image of what a gender-inclusive Christ-like attitude should be. Although Christ has always been God and the Son of God (v. 6), when he took on humanity, he voluntarily "made himself nothing" by taking on the very "nature" of a servant and was made in "human likeness" (v. 7). Yes, I know, he was also "found in appearance as a man" (v. 8), but the significance here lies in him being made in *human likeness*. It's worth noting that maleness, by itself, does not guarantee human likeness; he could have appeared as a male in the likeness of a goat or unicorn if he'd wanted. But only a perfect one of "us" could redeem the rest of the universally sinful, fallen "us." The eternal Creator God, the Christ, the Messiah, chose to become a fully human being. The only way other human beings would recognize him as human was for him to take on either the appearance of a man or a woman. And the only way the Jewish leaders would even take a second glance at him was if he was a man.

No doubt, Christ's maleness was at least symbolically essential in meeting priestly and sacrificial functions in a Jewish world, but his maleness did nothing more to guarantee forgiveness, Spirit-gifting and credentialing for the men of the world than it did for the women of the world. Nor did God the Father exalt his ever-existing Son to the highest place because he took on human maleness. He sits at the right hand of the Father as a representative of all *humankind*, whether expressed in maleness or femaleness. Adam was no less deserving of death, nor was Eve less worthy of life. The first male required redemption just as much as the first female, and every female or male since is guaranteed, upon confession, complete forgiveness and complete empowering for any ministry.

THESIS # 67

God, who is free to act according to his good purpose, may purpose to ordain whom he chooses.

Therefore, my dear friends, as you have always obeyed—not only in my presence, but now much more in my absence—continue to work out your salvation with fear and trembling, for it is God who works in you to will and to act according to his good purpose...as you hold out the word of life.

(Philippians 2:12–13, 16)

Paul is obviously writing to the entire Corinthian congregation, apparently treating men and women with equal importance. He calls them "my dear friends," not his dear male friends. Then he assures them all that it can only be the Creator-Redeemer-Messiah God who works in each of them (male or female) to exercise his will and actions *according to his good purpose*. When will we learn that only God decides when and who to call for any given ministry, and he does this "according to his good purpose," not according to any long-held, gender-specific, man-made protocol?

Two verses later (vv. 15–16) Paul calls the Philippian congregation faultless, blameless, pure children of God (nothing suggests that males were more faultless, blameless, etc.) living in a depraved generation, "in which you shine like stars in the universe *as you hold out the word of life.*" How could anyone possibly suggest that Paul is addressing the men in the congregation any differently than the women?

And how can "holding out" the word of life mean anything less than teaching or preaching?

THESIS # 68

To Paul, impressive religious credentials were meaningless compared to gaining a greater knowledge of God.

But whatever was to my profit I now consider loss for the sake of Christ. What is more, I consider everything a loss compared to the surpassing greatness of knowing Christ Jesus my Lord, for whose sake I have lost all things. I consider them rubbish, that I may gain Christ and be found in him, not having a righteousness of my own that comes from the law, but that which is through faith in Christ…Forgetting what is behind and straining toward what is ahead, I press on toward the goal to win the prize…All of us who are mature should take such a view of things. And if on some point you think differently, that too God will make clear to you. Only let us live up to what we have already attained.

(Philippians 3:7–9; 13, 15–16)

Jewish temple leadership required the "Right Stuff." A few verses earlier, Paul lists some essential credentials—all of which he held. Let's look at them in reverse order: he reminds his readers that he was faultless in his legalism, zealous in persecuting Christians, a Pharisee, a Hebrew of the Hebrews and a Benjamite from the people of Israel. What an amazing lineage and heritage! Surely, any Jewish synagogue would welcome his leadership. Actually, as impressive as Paul's portfolio sounds, it would be absolutely useless without one more requirement—the first and most important qualification of all—"circumcised on the eighth day" (v. 5). In one overarching, legalistic swoop, this male-only ritual trumped any other qualification, thereby prohibiting all women from Jewish leadership. In Craig Keener's book, *Paul, Women and Wives*, he says, "The rabbis clearly had it in for Eve." He also reminds us that, according to Jewish tradition, women marched ahead of the casket in a funeral procession because Eve brought death to the world, and the reason women menstruated was because Eve shed Adam's blood (114).

We must not lose sight of how immensely significant maleness was to Jewish religious leaders. For this reason, it seems even more significant that this impeccably qualified Jew would write: "But whatever was to my profit, I now consider loss for the sake of Christ." Surely, he includes circumcision—and even maleness—in the factors he now renounces. He considers *everything* a loss when he compares it to something far more important: "the surpassing greatness of knowing Christ Jesus my Lord." All of those credentials might help if he was still keeping the Law to accumulate a righteousness of his own (v. 9), but Paul gives all that up for "the righteousness that comes from God and is by faith."

If righteousness can only be achieved by *men* getting circumcised or keeping laws, then by all means, let's declare all women unrighteous forever! But ever since Christ's resurrection, the only way to be righteous is through faith in him. Perhaps this is what Paul is referring to when he says, "All of us who are mature should take such a view of things" (v. 15).

THESIS # 69

Paul calls Euodia and Syntyche his "fellow workers"— the same category as several other men.

I plead with Euodia and I plead with Syntyche to agree with each other in the Lord. Yes, and I ask you, loyal yokefellow, help these women who have contended at my side in the cause of the gospel, along with Clement and the rest of my fellow workers...

(Philippians 4:2–3)

Among the many situations Paul addresses in his letter to the church at Philippi, there is one pressing matter involving two high-profile women who apparently have some unsettled issues between them. He pleads with them to "be of the same mind in the Lord," and asks his unnamed "true companion" to help them resolve the conflict.

What I find interesting is that Paul includes these women in the same category as Clement and the rest of his "fellow workers" (v. 3). There seems to be a strong significance to the term "fellow workers" (TNIV uses "co-workers"). Bilezikian, among others, points out that when Paul uses this term it "seems to have become a technical label to designate people who identify closely with him in his church-planting efforts as front-line, pioneer missionaries" (198). Earlier in this letter, Paul uses the term for Epaphroditus (2:25), and elsewhere it is used for Timothy (Romans 16:21) and Titus (2 Corinthians 8:23). Note that Paul also points out that the two Philippian women "contended at my side in the cause of the gospel" (v. 3). Whatever ministry they had, one can assume it was more significant than many contemporary women are offered. Compare this to Thesis # 28.

THESIS # 70

If teaching and wisdom make a person "perfect in Christ," then wise, well-taught women should be equally qualified vessels.

We proclaim him, admonishing and teaching everyone with all wisdom, so that we may present everyone perfect in Christ. To this end I labor, struggling with all his energy, which so powerfully works in me.

(Colossians 1:28–29)

The above verses clearly speak for themselves. Paul has just explained that God has commissioned him to present the word of God "in its fullness"—referring to the finished work of Christ, which he calls the "mystery" that is finally revealed to the Gentiles. That mystery, simply put, is "Christ in you, the hope of glory" v. 27).

Paul says he and Timothy proclaim Christ by "admonishing and teaching everyone with all wisdom." They admonish and teach *everyone*. The wisdom of this mystery is carefully taught to men and women. Their goal in doing this is to present *everyone* "perfect in Christ" (v. 28) or, as the TNIV says, "fully mature" in Christ. He then adds that he labors, struggling with all the energy of Christ which powerfully works in him.

How else can you interpret what Paul is saying? Surely he's not suggesting special classes for the men so that they may be fully mature. No, Paul has committed his life to passing on the knowledge of the "mystery" that Christ can actually live in and powerfully work through every man and woman, making them all fully mature in Christ.

THESIS # 71

By Christ's death on the cross, both men and women have been set free from the Jewish "written code" and regulations.

He forgave us all our sins, having cancelled the written code with its regulations...he took it away, nailing it to the cross. And having disarmed the powers and authorities, he made a public spectacle of them, triumphing over them by the cross....Since you died with Christ to the basic principles of this world, why, as though you still belonged to it, do you submit to its rules...?...For you died, and your life is now hidden with Christ in God.

(excerpts—Colossians 2:13–14, 20–3:3)

Many scholarly books plumb the theological depths of this amazing chapter. Paul warns the congregation at Colosse not to be taken captive by "deceptive philosophy" founded on the "basic principles of this world" rather than on Christ (v. 8), because we have all received "fullness in Christ" (v. 9). He further explains that all followers of Christ have received a spiritual circumcision (v. 11)—which, of course, applies equally to women and men—and have been made alive with Christ, who has "cancelled the written code" (v. 14). This last phrase makes more sense in the TNIV: "having cancelled the charge of our legal indebtedness." In short, when Christ died on the cross, any Old Testament law that would previously have condemned a man or woman became powerless through his death. And at that moment, Christ triumphed over whatever curses men and religions have caused women to bear for the last two thousand years.

Finally, Paul brings us to a logical conclusion: Since Christ's death also brought death to legalistic laws which were "based on human commands and teachings" (v. 22), why do we allow man-made laws to keep dictating what we can or cannot do? We are now "raised with Christ" and our hearts and minds are set on things above (3:1–3). Every man now has full right and authority to pastor, teach or lead, based solely on Christ's cancellation of his indebtedness to God. Yet, in many instances, male church leaders still allow the cloud of that indebtedness to remain over women.

THESIS # 72

Paul lists many requirements for Colossian church leaders who teach and admonish; gender is not one of them.

Since, then, you have been raised with Christ…whatever you do, whether in word or deed, do it all in the name of the Lord Jesus, giving thanks to the Father through him.

(Colossians 3:1, 17)

97

Please open your Bible to Colossians 3:1–17 (not just the two partial verses above) as you consider the following comments. Ironically, I happen to be writing this on New Year's Day, the day most of us announce—or at least dreamingly think about—life-changing resolutions for the coming year. Suppose your Pastor and church leadership were to resolve to use the occasion to encourage your flock to grow deeper spiritually. They set aside the first six months of Sunday mornings for sermons specifically on this passage. The Pastor informs your congregation that he and the board of elders will be watching for spiritual growth as the "truth of the Word" changes hearts. At the end of the series, those who evidence the greatest maturity will be invited to take on deeper ministry responsibilities. The Pastor's twenty-five or so verse-by-verse sermons from this passage will cover the following points, taken directly from the first seventeen verses of Colossians 3:

1. Set your hearts and minds on things above.

2. Put to death all "earthly nature" sins (sexual impurity, lust, greed).

3. Rid yourselves of anger, rage, malice, slander, filthy language.

4. Do not lie to each other.

5. Put off old self, put on new self in the image of its Creator.

6. Practice no class distinctions (race, circumcision, etc.).

7. Clothe yourselves with compassion, kindness, etc.

8. Bear with and forgive each other.

9. Over all these virtues put on love.

10. Let the peace of Christ rule in your hearts—all one body.

11. Let the word of Christ dwell in you richly.

12. (as you) Teach and admonish one another with all wisdom.

13. (as you) Sing psalms, hymns, spiritual songs with gratitude in your heart.

14. Whatever you do (words or deeds), do all in the name of the Lord Jesus.

15. Give thanks to God the Father through Christ.

Now, fast-forward to June. Before your Pastor and the board of elders leave for summer vacation, they meet to review the results of the sermon series and decide to send a confidential letter to—oh, let's say—the five men and five women who have shown the most spiritual growth. The five men receive a letter of congratulation and encouragement in which the following sentence appears: "The church leadership team is very excited about the obvious growth we have seen in your life as a result of the recent sermon series, and we invite you to serve on our Elder's Council in the coming year and to consider teaching an adult Bible class and/or occasionally preaching in the Pastor's absence."

The five women also receive a letter of congratulation and encouragement in which the following sentence appears: "The church leadership team is very excited about the obvious growth we have seen in your life as a result of the recent sermon series, and we invite you to serve on our Worship and Music committee this coming year and to consider joining the 'Morning Out for Moms' team or our Prayer Chain ministry."

Why should women sit through six months of sermons on spiritual maturity and only be offered "M.O.M.s" and Music while the men are given the heavy-duty positions? Take another look at the fifteen points. Nowhere does Paul say, "Point # 12 is for men only, but there's lots of other neat stuff that women can do (# 13, for instance)." Neither point # 12 nor # 13 is meant to be a prize to hand out for spiritual growth or gender; these are actions the entire Christian church should always be doing. As men and women do these actions (teach, admonish, sing psalms, hymns—or whatever they do) they must keep becoming more mature, keep practicing the other points and, above all, keep letting the "word of Christ" dwell in them richly (v. 16) as they keep giving thanks to God the Father for the privilege of ministry that neither gender deserves.

THESIS # 73

The God who transformed Saul into Paul can surely transform women into church elders or pastors.

I thank Christ Jesus our Lord, who has given me strength, that he considered me faithful, appointing me to his service. Even though I was once a blasphemer and a persecutor and a violent man, I was shown mercy because I acted in ignorance and unbelief. . . . I was shown mercy so that in me, the worst of sinners, Christ Jesus might display his unlimited patience as an example for those who would believe...

(1 Timothy 1:12–13, 16)

This passage literally preaches itself. Paul lists some pretty obvious reasons why Christ would pass him by and choose someone else to be his missionary or to author most of the books in the New Testament. When he was known as Saul, he was a violent blasphemer who persecuted Christians. By his own testimony he was the "worst of sinners." Why would God dig so deep in the barrel to find this loser when there had to be better qualified men out there? If anyone's sin was bad enough to keep God from using him, it would certainly be Saul. But the new "Paul" humbly explains how it happened: Christ gave him strength, considered him faithful, appointed him to service, showed him mercy because of his ignorance and unbelief and displayed his unlimited patience through him.

Why don't churches use women in leadership positions? Is it because they're too sinful? Paul says he was even worse than the worst of sinners. Is it because they don't deserve it? Paul didn't either. Is it because they sinned ignorantly? Christ will show them mercy.

THESIS # 74

Although Paul states that it is imperative that women be taught, the object of their submission in this case may be their instructors, not their husbands.

A woman should learn in quietness and full submission.

(1 Timothy 2:11)

If the apostle Paul were still alive, I would ask him exactly what he meant by the above sentence. Traditionally, this verse has been an important part of the hierarchical arsenal against women's admission into theological education and ordination—sort of a carryover of the Jewish practice not to permit women to study the Torah. So, for thousands of years, women have been told to be quiet and submissive.

There are many diverse and complicated interpretations of what Paul was trying to say here. In fact, Paul may have really meant it as a command for all time: "Women, stay quiet and submissive. Leave the learning and teaching to men. Forever." However, if that is the real message, it disagrees strongly with almost everything Paul said or practiced. Some of the confusion may connect to a Greek word Paul uses: *manthaneton*—which means 'learn' or 'be taught.' Paul uses the word here in what is called the *imperative* mood, which is usually translated as a command. He is not saying, "I command women to be silent and submissive," but rather, "*I command that women be taught.*"

His call for women's submission is likely referring to submission to the pastor-teacher in this case, not their husbands—something any teacher of his day would expect from students.

THESIS # 75

If women are allowed to teach, their teaching is also authoritative.

I do not permit a woman to teach or to have authority over a man; she must be silent.

(1 Timothy 2:12)

Many Christians believe that women may talk in church, but must never preach or teach—especially if men are present. Thomas Schreiner's restrictions on women are obvious: "…it is appropriate for women who travel as speakers to address a mixed audience as articulate and thoughtful *representatives of a feminine perspective on many experiences of life*" (223, emphasis mine). No preaching—just share your experiences from a feminine perspective! Many chapters, indeed entire books, have been written, centered on this one verse and/or passage. If you want to dig into this deeply, you should pick up a copy of Richard and Catherine Clark Kroeger's *I Suffer Not a Woman,* where they record impressive historical and archaeological data relating to 1 Timothy 2:11–15. Chapter 3 of Craig Keener's *Paul, Women and Wives* also gives an excellent overview of various interpretations of this passage (the entire book is great). The Christian community should be grateful for the outstanding academia many authors have contributed to this topic.

Meanwhile, here are some very simple observations from this verse. When Paul tells Timothy, "I do not permit a woman to teach or have authority over a man," he says it in the *present* tense. In other words, it can be (but doesn't have to be) translated, "I *presently* do not permit a woman to teach or have authority over a man." In those days, most teaching—at least in areas of theology, philosophy, medicine or law—was only available to men and done by men. It would be natural for emerging congregations to turn to qualified men when seeking leaders. So, one of many possibilities would be that Paul is suggesting something like this: "It is imperative that women now be taught, but until they learn, they should remain silent and submissively learn from those who are already well informed in these areas."

This still leaves the issue of women having authority over men. Keener offers three possibilities for the meaning of this Greek verb, *authentein*—(1) to accept a position of authority, (2) to seize authority in an "overbearing way," or (3) to proclaim oneself as the originator of authority (108). The Kroegers favor the third option, adding that Paul may be speaking against Gnostic or proto-Gnostic mythology glorifying Eve (117). Any or all of the above options may have merit, but I'd like to think the whole discussion could be much simpler.

Maybe Paul is just pointing out that the role of teaching automatically carries with it some degree of authority. From first grade on, a child will believe something because "Teacher said so!" However, in teaching biblical truth, the authority does not come from the teacher (male or female) but from the Scriptures he or she is teaching (Liefeld, 146). Perhaps this is why Paul tells his young apprentice Timothy to devote himself to the "public reading of Scripture" (1 Timothy 4:13) and, in his second letter, to "Preach the *Word*"—the obvious authority behind all church teaching (2 Timothy 4:2), especially if it's being taught by a young pastor still wet behind the ears (1 Timothy 4:12) or a woman, who up until then, would only have felt free to share her "feminine perspective."

THESIS # 76

The common assumption that men have authority over women because Adam was created first has no biblical justification.

For Adam was formed first, then Eve.

(1 Timothy 2:13)

Obviously, hierarchicalists sharply disagree with this thesis statement. For instance, it is no surprise that Larry Christensen insists on a woman's subordination to her husband: "This subordination is grounded upon the creation. 'Adam was formed first, then Eve'" (39). A decade later, James Hurley uses this passage to teach that "men rather than women should teach and exercise authority in the church" (207). This is still a very popular interpretation, as frequently articulated by Piper and Grudem, who state as a "fact" that Adam "is called to bear the responsibility of headship." They further state, "That *fact* is validated by the New Testament when Paul uses the *fact* that 'Adam was formed first, then Eve' (1 Timothy 2:13) to draw a *conclusion* about male leadership in the church" (81, emphasis mine).

In recent years, more and more authors have come to question these "facts" and "conclusions." Just because Paul writes, "Adam was created *first, then* Eve," it does not automatically follow that Adam had been given greater leadership or authority. Linda Belleville suggests, "'First-then' defines a temporal sequence, without implying either ontological or functional property" (222). Just because I shave *first* and *then* brush my teeth does not mean that shaving is more important. On the other hand, Paul might have had another significant reason to purposely state that Adam was created first, perhaps to stamp out pre-Gnostic teaching that touted the superiority of Eve over Adam and sought to validate her supposed connection to "goddess worship" (Kroeger and Kroeger, 105). Arden Thiessen also devotes a few pages to the pre-Gnostic influence, concluding: "The best way to make sense of the theology of these letters is to assume the apostle is dealing here with a cultic perversion not found elsewhere" (151). There is still no possible way to prove that Paul's reason for writing this sentence was to show Adam's superiority. The discussion continues into the next two theses.

THESIS # 77

When tempted by the Devil, Eve sins; yet, Adam also sins— even without the satanic deception that Eve had to face.

And Adam was not the one deceived; it was the woman who was deceived and became a sinner.

(1 Timothy 2:14)

Historically, this verse has been interpreted to show how fickle Eve was because she was so easily deceived by Satan; hence, women can never be given positions of leadership or responsibility. Even today, there are many leading scholars who still interpret this verse this way. For instance, commenting on this very verse, J. N. D. Kelly states: "[Paul's] point is that since Eve was so gullible a victim of the serpent's wiles, she clearly cannot be trusted to teach" (68). Similarly, Ralph Earle writes, "It was the woman who was deceived by Satan and who disobeyed God.…Since she was so easily deceived she should not be trusted as a teacher" (362). Robert D. Culver dogmatically affirms, "The catastrophe of Eden is the beacon for all generations when the sexes repeat the folly of Eve and Adam, and exchange their distinctive position and function" (37).

The whole point here is that Eve had to face the Deceiver— Satan, the Devil—the smoothest and most sophisticated deceiver this world will ever know. What's Adam's excuse? No one deceived him, but he still chose to disobey God. I applaud Gretchen Gaebelein Hull's comment on this verse: "One severe logical difficulty with 1 Timothy 2:13–14 is why a deliberate sinner (Adam) would be better qualified to teach than a deceived person (Eve)" (*Equal*, 186— Compare Theses 7–9 on Genesis 3).

THESIS # 78

A woman's salvation does not come through keeping house and bearing children.

But women will be saved through childbearing—if they continue in faith, love and holiness with propriety.

(1 Timothy 2:15)

Whatever the above phrase means ("women will be saved through childbearing"), it cannot mean that the only way a woman is to experience eternal life is to give birth! Some authors suggest that women will receive salvation through living a "holy" life and living up to the standard of domestic "propriety" of cultured women in Paul's day. Others feel it is simply saying that Christian women will be saved from the "curse" of painful childbirth through Christ's redemption. Regardless, the answer must obviously apply to all females, whether single or married, with or without children.

Paul says that women will be saved (or restored) by *the* childbearing (note definite article), or even "the birth of *the* child" (both are possible translations). In other words, Paul may be suggesting to Timothy that Christ's redemption ended (nullified) the long-held position of subservience, even slavery, that women endured both in secular and Jewish cultures, and in light of this, it was now time for the new Christian community to ensure that women received the same redemptive benefits that all men (Jew-Gentile, slave-free, etc.) already enjoyed.

It comes as no surprise that there is no single convincing interpretation of this verse that pleases everyone. Christians have vehemently fought over this topic for over two thousand years. What follows is my personal slant on the issue. Let's pretend that when Timothy received this letter from Paul, even he couldn't figure out what Paul meant. So—let's pretend—that he wrote back: "Paul, would you please carefully go through [what we now call] verses 11–15 of your second chapter—line by line—and add explanatory comments? I need to know what was going on in your head." Now, let's pretend that what follows each italicized scriptural phrase is Paul's explanation of its meaning. Remember, the operative word here is "pretend."

"A woman should learn in quietness and full submission."

Tim, because women have never been taught, they are prime targets for false teachers [see 2 Timothy 3:6]. It is imperative that they be given opportunity to learn, but they should do so quietly, submitting themselves to the instructor.

"I do not permit a woman to teach or have authority over a man; she must be silent."

Until women are taught, I am presently not permitting them to authoritatively teach men who have had years of learning. They should be silent until qualified to speak.

"For Adam was formed first, then Eve."

You have to remember, Tim, over the years women have been handicapped because of their lack of knowledge, just as Eve was. *"Adam was created first,"* so it was only Adam who heard that powerful directive from God about what not to eat in the garden. Then God created Eve. Adam (supposedly) passed on the "eating instructions" to her, but it lacked the impact of her hearing it directly from Jehovah.

"And Adam was not the one deceived."

In other words, Satan (the Great Deceiver) didn't even try to deceive Adam. He probably heard the conversations Adam and God had, and knew how serious God was about that tree.

"...it was the woman who was deceived and became a sinner."

As usual, Satan knew what he was doing: he went after the one with less knowledge. Adam and God had talked a lot already—Adam had even named all the animals. Then naïve Eve came along and Satan seized the opportunity to challenge her knowledge ("Did God really say you must not eat? How can you be sure? You weren't there!"). She became a sinner by yielding to deception, but what about Adam? He didn't have to face the Deceiver—he chose to sin with his eyes wide open!

"But women will be saved through childbearing—if they continue in faith, love and holiness with propriety."

Obviously, I don't mean that every woman has to bear a child to gain eternal life. I'm talking about the most significant "childbearing" that ever took place: Mary giving birth to Jesus, the Christ. Whatever or whoever the Deceiver ruined, the Redeemer rescued! But, just as with men, redemption is to be followed by a life of faith, love and appropriate conduct.

THESIS # 79

In listing qualifications for overseers and deacons, Paul's use of the male pronoun does not limit these offices to men.

Here is a trustworthy saying: If anyone sets his heart on being an overseer, he desires a noble task.

(1 Timothy 3:1)

Anyone means *anyone*. The Greek word *tis* is used for both genders. Anyone can desire to be an overseer. The only qualifications are *desire* plus certain attributes, not *gender* plus certain attributes. The TNIV makes this clearer: "*Whoever* aspires to be an overseer…" Enough said.

THESIS # 80

One's appointment to a position of spiritual leadership must be based solely on qualifications and character, not gender.

Now the overseer must be above reproach, the husband of but one wife, temperate, self-controlled, respectable, hospitable, able to teach, not given to drunkenness, not violent but gentle, not quarrelsome, not a lover of money. He must mange his own family well.

(1 Timothy 3:2–4a)

Throughout Scripture, unless gender must be specifically spelled out for some reason, the masculine gender becomes the "default" gender. In other words, "husband of but one wife" could also be said "wife of but one husband" (although, this would perhaps be considered culturally insensitive), and "he" can refer to "she." I see nothing stopping a woman *with the above qualifications* from holding any office in any church.

THESIS # 81

Followers of strict legalism are often blind to the good in all of God's creation.

They forbid people to marry and order them to abstain from certain foods, which God created to be received with thanksgiving by those who believe and who know the truth. For everything God created is good, and nothing is to be rejected if it is received with thanksgiving, because it is consecrated by the word of God and prayer.

(1 Timothy 4:3–5)

In 1 Timothy 4 Paul is warning Timothy that there are a lot of teachers out there who have abandoned "the faith" and are following after deceiving spirits and "things taught by demons" (v. 1). As a result, they teach lies, demand celibacy—even abstention from certain foods and marriage. Paul's warning should still be heeded in our day. Just because someone is teaching something, there's no guarantee of the individual's upright motives or the truth of what is being taught. Remember, Peter's "sheet vision" (Acts 10, Thesis # 24) taught him that all food and all nationalities are to be accepted, contrary to Jewish teaching.

I don't think all pastors who promote male superiority are false teachers and liars. I do think that many of them might have been incorrectly taught the hierarchical view without also having taken the time to prayerfully and seriously study the issues for themselves. Verse 4 clearly says "For everything God created is *good*." Pure simple logic would then ask, "Did God create woman?" Yes. Well, then, women are good. In fact, it was only after God created both Adam and Eve that he declared what he had created was "very good" (Genesis 1:31). I long to see the day when God's worldwide church will consecrate their women for all ministries "by the Word of God and prayer" and gratefully embrace and "receive with thanksgiving" the manifold blessings these women will contribute.

THESIS # 82

Passion, commitment and proven ability to minister God's word are the hallmarks of those God calls to minister.

Do your best to present yourself to God as one approved, a workman who does not need to be ashamed and who correctly handles the word of truth.

(2 Timothy 2:15)

Paul is addressing this letter to a man—his apprentice, young Timothy, but I'm pretty sure that Paul would say the same thing to a young woman who is seeking God's call on her life. However, if a young woman in some congregations—even today—shows that she can "correctly handle the word of truth," she is still not accepted in a teaching/preaching position. Yet, a qualified man would be approved for the same types of ministry. The word "man" in this verse carries no gender; "worker," as in TNIV, is more accurate.

The New Testament is full of passionate pleas calling Christian congregations to higher levels of spirituality. None of them are specifically addressed to men, even though this one is written to a specific man (Luke also wrote the book of Acts to a specific man, Theophilus). Even so, we continue to superimpose our gender grid over each ministry, concluding that only men are capable of correctly handling the Word of Truth. Apparently, a woman "doing her best" is not good enough.

THESIS # 83

Believers, like household vessels, must be clean before they can be used.

In a large house there are articles not only of gold and silver, but also of wood and clay; some are for noble purposes and some for ignoble. If a man cleanses himself from the latter, he will be an instrument for noble purposes, made holy, useful to the Master and prepared to do any good work.

(2 Timothy 2:20–21)

Much of this thesis statement is a mirror image of the previous one. It is also similar to Theses #35 and #36. In 1 Corinthians 12 Paul explains that some parts of our bodies are more important than others. If Paul were writing to Timothy today, he might explain that every house has some very valuable dishes as well as cracked, stained, plastic ones. Generally speaking, the gold or crystal dishes are regularly cleaned and polished, while the junky, dirty ones might sit under a potted plant or be used as an ash tray for years. But both plastic dishes and lead crystal goblets have the potential to get dirty or to stay clean; the choice is up to the owner. The difference with human beings is that we (the dishes) are also the owners of the dishes (our bodies). If we make the choice to keep our "dish" clean, God can use us for noble purposes—regardless of whether we are crystal or plastic! What we *cannot* choose is whether we are male or female (at least, not without some pretty serious and controversial surgery!).

Paul is writing to a male (Timothy), and most translations read, "If a *man* cleanses *himself*..." There is no gender in this statement—the TNIV says *"Those* who cleanse *themselves*..."*—so if a woman cleanses herself, will she also be an instrument for "noble purposes?" Will she be made just as holy and prepared to do "any good work" as a man would be? Or does her cleansing and preparation permit only *some* good works?

THESIS # 84

When we discourage any believer from studying and applying Scripture, we are responsible for his or her spiritual weakness.

All Scripture is God-breathed and is useful for teaching, rebuking, correcting and training in righteousness, so that the man of God may be thoroughly equipped for every good work.

(2 Timothy 3:16–17)

This third chapter of 2 Timothy divides nicely into four interrelated sections. If we understand the first three, then the verse above will take on greater meaning. Section # 1 (vv. 1–5) is a terrifying but accurate prediction Paul makes about how our world will look in the "last days" before Christ's return. People will demand self-gratification, abuse others and be disobedient to parents, not self-controlled, haters of good and of God, etc. The surprising thing is that they will still have "a form of godliness," even though they deny its power. Section # 2 begins with v. 6, where Paul compares these last-day reprobates to the false and devious teachers of his day who preyed on "weak-willed" women who scramble after every new doctrine that comes along, and were "always learning but never able to acknowledge the truth" (v. 7—compare 2 Peter 3:10–18).

In the third section, Paul contrasts these first two scenarios with that of his young apprentice, Timothy. What a difference! First, Paul reminds Timothy of how he was carefully nurtured in the faith by his mother Eunice and his grandmother Lois (2 Timothy 1:5). He has known Paul's teaching, way of life, purpose, faith, patience, love, etc. (3:10). Built on that foundation, he encourages Timothy to "continue in what you have learned," and reminds him that "from infancy you have known the holy Scriptures." This prepares us for section # 4 (v. 16).

If Scripture had never recorded the first 15 verses of chapter 3, we might never have appreciated how important v. 16 really is. It sounds like Paul purposely sets the scene to make his young apprentice listen up. "Timothy, *mark this:* (1) Someday the world is going to get much, much worse; (2) even now, we see false teachers seducing untaught, easily swayed women who will fall for anything; (3) be thankful you've had sound teaching all your life; and (4) that's why you must keep studying Scripture so that, no matter what happens, you will be thoroughly equipped for every good work."

There is an application here to how we handle gender differences in our churches today. As our world continues its moral disintegration, we have a solemn responsibility to encourage women to study the Scriptures with the goal of being equipped for "every good work" and to ensure they have ministry opportunities equal to those offered to men. If we do not, by default we discourage many women from their highest potential and calling, deprive the church of a vast army of gifted, qualified leaders and handicap the body of Christ in its most needed hour.

THESIS # 85

The purpose of men and women receiving solid teaching is to equip them to "encourage others by sound doctrine."

He must hold firmly to the trustworthy message as it has been taught, so that he can encourage others by sound doctrine and refute those who oppose it.

(Titus 1:9)

I memorized this verse forty-nine years ago, the year that I entered Winnipeg Bible Institute, now known as Providence College and Seminary in Otterburne, Manitoba, Canada. Old-timers reading this book may, like me, still remember Titus 1:9 in the weighty words of the King James Version: "Holding fast the faithful word as he hath been taught that he may be able by sound doctrine both to exhort and to convince the gainsayers." Translations change, and so they should, but many times during my four decades of pulpit ministry, those familiar words would echo in my ears as I prepared a sermon or defended some doctrinal truth.

There weren't as many female students at WBI then, but I'll never forget the day we began our first "Systematic Theology" class of about fifteen men and one woman. The instructor welcomed us all to the class, especially the sole female representative. With much graciousness and tongue-in-cheek humor, he said to her, "Men have theological minds; women have devotional minds." We all laughed— so did she. But on the last day of class, as the instructor handed out the grades, he also invited us to applaud the person who received the highest grade—the woman with the "devotional" mind.

As in the previous two theses, I am sure that Paul is not just writing this epistle to Titus, but expects its content to apply to us all. I am thankful for the thousands of committed women who are now graduating from excellent seminaries with post-graduate degrees in every related academic discipline, prepared and confident to "encourage others by sound doctrine" and highly capable to "refute those who oppose it." Unfortunately, it is still true that men with the same degrees—and often lower grades —are much more likely to be ordained and invited to use their skills in more significant ways.

THESIS # 86

As with the issue of slavery, the role of women must be interpreted in light of first century culture.

Likewise, teach the older women to be reverent in the way they live, not to be slanderers or addicted to much wine, but to teach what is good. Then they can train the younger women to love their husbands and children, to be self controlled and pure, to be busy at home, to be kind, and to be subject to their husbands, so that no one will malign the word of God.

(Titus 2:3–5)

At first glance, these verses certainly read like a hierarchical application of Scripture, but let's look at some of the less obvious factors. As you read through this short letter, it doesn't take much time or education to see that there is one primary attribute that Paul desires for Titus, his "true son in our common faith" (1:4); that is, *self-control.* Paul uses the term five times in the forty-six verses that make up this letter. Self-control is recommended for aspiring elders (1:8), older men (2:2), young women (2:5), young men (2:6) and the church in general (2:12). Paul recognizes that the early Christian church is surrounded by false teachers who, Paul says, are "detestable, disobedient and unfit for doing anything good" (1:16). With this fledgling church constantly under the critical eye of a pagan world, Paul calls for self-control in every situation, but within the preservation of that society's norms and standards.

In this context, Paul also exhorts young wives to be subject to their husbands (2:5). Does this mean that Paul advocates unequivocal submission from every wife to her husband's every whim and fancy? Of course not. His advice sounds more like the old saying, "When in Rome, do as the Romans do." In the same way, he tells slaves to put up with slavery, so that their attitude to their master "will make the teaching about God our Savior attractive" (2:10). In a hierarchical, male-dominant master-slave society, sometimes submission to one's condition has a better testimony than anarchy. More on this in Thesis # 90.

THESIS # 87

Jesus Christ, our high priest and perfect sacrifice, offers every believer greater ministries than performed by any Old Testament high priest.

The blood of goats and bulls and the ashes of a heifer sprinkled on those who are ceremonially unclean sanctify them so that they are outwardly clean. How much more, then, will the blood of Christ, who through the eternal Spirit offered himself unblemished to God, cleanse our consciences from acts that lead to death, so that we may serve the living God!

(Hebrews 9:13–14)

The worst assignment I was ever given in seminary was part of a class on the book of Hebrews. The professor announced that one-third of our final grade would be offered to any student who signed a form declaring that s/he had read the entire book of Hebrews five times— *out loud!* In retrospect, that might also have been the most valuable

assignment I ever received in seminary. If you really want to understand how Christ's sacrifice of himself compares to the Old Testament legalistic sacrificial system, read the book of Hebrews five times
out loud. Saturate yourself with its profound simplicity. Be forever
amazed at "*how much more*" Jesus Christ accomplished compared to
what the Law could do. The contrast between v. 13 and v. 14 in the
passage above is staggering. It reminds me of what Paul says in Romans 8:3: "For what the law was powerless to do…God did by sending his own Son." Now that our conscience has been cleansed, we are
free to "serve the living God!" (v. 14).

This leaves the ever haunting question: Just *how much more* did
Christ accomplish? Did he accomplish as much for women as he did
for men? If, indeed, we all (male and female) now "have confidence
to enter the Most Holy Place" (Hebrews 10:19)—that sanctuary reserved only for high priests on rare occasions—why do many women
still not have confidence to enter our pulpits and serve at our communion tables?

THESIS # 88

All believers become equal members of Christ's "royal priesthood" in order that they may declare his praises.

*You also, like living stones, are being built into a spiritual house to be a
holy priesthood, offering spiritual sacrifices acceptable to God through
Jesus Christ. . . . But you are a chosen people, a royal priesthood, a holy
nation, a people belonging to God, that you may declare the praises of
him who called you out of darkness into his wonderful light.*

(1 Peter 2:5, 9)

This sounds like the book of Hebrews, doesn't it? Peter tells us that
when any person becomes a true Christian, that person becomes
much like the temple's sacrificial system, only better. We are not the

real stones that the temple was made of, and we're not real Old Testament priests. Rather, we are spiritual stones, being built into a spiritual temple that can continually offer spiritual sacrifices that are acceptable to God! We don't approach God just once a year with a dead animal. Whatever the sacrificial system required, the once-dead-but-now-resurrected Christ has met fully for us, and he calls us his "chosen people" and "*royal priesthood.*"

Why is this so important? Because many who hold to the hierarchical model consider that the role of high priest in the Old Testament is now replaced by certain male-only offices in the church (some even insist that husbands fulfill a priestly role in their homes). In *The Ordination of Women*, Paul Jewett writes, "As it was unthinkable that a female should be a priest in Israel, so it is unthinkable that a woman should be a minister in the church, inasmuch as Christians are spiritual Levites and the church, the new Israel of God" (15). However, Peter declares that we are all (males—even Peter—and females) a royal priesthood; God accepts all of our sacrifices and invites us all to declare his praises. As Susan Foh argues, "There is no continuity between the office of priest, which ceased when Christ sacrificed himself once for all (Hebrews 7:11–10:25), and the office of elder or pastor-teacher....Women are priests in these senses just as men, but the status does not qualify any one for church office" (93–94). In other words, whether male or female, we are all priests, and, whether male or female, some of us may become pastors or elders.

THESIS # 89

As is often repeated in the New Testament, the primary requirement for involvement in ministry is purity, not gender.

Dear friends, I urge you, as aliens and strangers in the world, to abstain from sinful desires, which war against the soul. Live such good lives among the pagans that, though they accuse you of doing wrong, they may see your good deeds and glorify God on the day he visits us.

(1 Peter 2:11–12)

This passage reinforces what we've been saying all along: the most important qualification for being a servant of God will always be the purity of one's life. People who don't go to church couldn't care less if the message is preached by an uneducated woman or an ordained man with a doctorate. The real qualification in their minds is the purity and sincerity of the messenger. (By the way, when you're trying to reach unchurched people, try explaining to them why a woman can't be an elder or serve communion in your church. Don't be surprised if it doesn't make sense to them.)

THESIS # 90

The practice of one-sided submission of wives to husbands is a man-made institution still prevalent in many cultures.

Submit your selves for the Lord's sake to every authority instituted among men…Slaves, submit yourselves to your masters…Wives, in the same way be submissive to your husbands...

(1 Peter 2:13, 18; 3:1)

"The world is watching!" This seems to be Peter's emphasis as he advises us on how important it is to keep the regulations in the society in which we live. First, there seems to be an overall heading in which we are admonished, for the Lord's sake, to submit ourselves to "every authority instituted among men," kings and governors being just two examples (vv. 13–14). Then we are given a few other general instructions: "Show proper respect to everyone. Love the brotherhood of believers, fear God, honor the king" (v. 17). In other words,

119

live by the laws of your land and keep the rules that have wisely been set down.

Peter then goes into detail about two particular practices of the day: slavery and wives' submission to husbands. If you are a Christian slave in a non-Christian society that endorses slavery, the best way to conduct yourself is carefully spelled out for you (vv. 18–21). In I. Howard Marshall's words, "An insubordinate wife was a bad witness for the gospel in any situation where non-Christian husbands expected subordination" (192). But what if circumstances and societal norms change? What if, one day, the government tells you that slaves are now free? Are you going to stay in slavery because "The Bible says…?" Indeed, these very biblical instructions continued to hinder the emancipation of slaves in many countries because well-meaning Christian leaders saw slavery as a God-given absolute for all time in every society.

So, what are we to do with 1 Peter 3:1? It says, "Wives, submit to your husbands," and spends six verses telling them how to do it. But what should wives do if they now live in a society that, by act of government, makes it law that men and women be treated equally? Hierarchicalists argue that wives' submission to husbands transcends all man-made rules and is based either on God's plan of creation or on Eve's causing Adam to sin. I find a little phrase in 3:1 interesting: "*In the same way*…." What can that possibly mean? In the same way as what? It might (and probably does) mean, in the same way as Christ bore our sins (vv. 24–25). But perhaps it refers back to v. 13: just as slavery is a man-made institution, perhaps wives' submission to husbands is also a man-made institution. If so, Paul may be suggesting that, *in the same way* as slavery is no longer appropriate, future societies (ours?) may one day eradicate gender inequality.

THESIS # 91

Peter's description of women as "weaker partners" does not disqualify them from any level of ministry.

Husbands, in the same way be considerate as you live with your wives, and treat them with respect as the weaker partner and as heirs with you of the gracious gift of life, so that nothing will hinder your prayers.

(1 Peter 3:7)

People who consider that women are somehow inferior to men often raise the "weaker partner" argument from the above verse. Indeed, if you interpret the 1 Timothy 2 passage to mean that women cannot teach or be in authority because Eve bungled everything and led Adam astray, it follows that women are flawed in some way and just not as strong willed, logical or intelligent as men are. Earlier, in Thesis # 9, I quoted Christensen saying that a woman "is more easily discouraged and dejected. God has made her that way" (127). Regarding a woman's vulnerability, Christensen also believes that a woman is vulnerable "at the emotional, psychological, and spiritual level. Here, too, she needs a husband's authority and protection" (35).

Gregg Johnson offers similar signs of women's "weaknesses," at least in positions of leadership and authority, stating, "They have physiologies and temperament traits that prepare them uniquely for childcare." He further argues that breaches of relationship and inability to have children are "common sources of feminine stress" (292). The implication might be: how can a woman be a good leader if she can't even handle simple domestic stress? His research on men suggests that "the more lateralized male brain would be expected to be more single-minded, focused, less distractible"—traits that apparently endow men with a more "competitive, goal-setting, rule-making, hierarchical approach to social interaction" (289-290).

So, what is the message Peter wants us to get from this? I think he is saying three things to men: (a) be considerate of your wives, (b) treat them with respect, and (c) treat them as heirs with you of the gracious gift of life. Any man in that day who heard Peter's words would have been astounded! After all, this is *Peter* talking—the rough and tumble fisherman who knew all too well how other lower-class men treated their wives. Chances are, they had never heard anyone talk this kindly about women. Imagine! He even tells these men to be "considerate." At least one translation (NASB) uses "understanding." The Greek word can also be translated as "knowledgeable." Husbands, know and understand your wives! And the main thing we should understand is that women in general are not as physically strong as men. That's all. As Edwin Blum, along with many others, points out in his commentary on 1 Peter, the only way women are weaker than men is physically, not "morally, spiritually or intellectually" (237). What's more, there are actually a few ways most women *are* physically stronger than men (childbirth comes to mind).

But Peter isn't finished. He now tells these men (and us) to treat their wives with "respect." This Greek word, *timee*, has several shades of meaning. In the old KJV it is translated 'honor' over 50 times, which is also the favorite word for the NIV. Several times in the New Testament we are told to honor our father and mother and to honor one another above ourselves (Romans 12:10). Peter also tells us to honor the king (1 Peter 2:17), and the book of Revelation is full of instances when we all bring "glory and *honor*" to God (4:9; 5:12, etc.). Finally, the word is also translated 'precious,' referring to Christ as the "precious cornerstone" (1 Peter 2:6).

It's time we started treating our wives as precious, honoring them above ourselves and always treating them with respect. Why? Because everything God did for us, he did for them, making them co-equal heirs with us of the "gracious gift of life."

THESIS # 92

God's "divine power" is obviously just as available to women as men.

His divine power has given us everything we need for life and godliness through our knowledge of him who called us by his own glory and goodness. Through these he has given us his very great and precious promises, so that through them you may participate in the divine nature and escape the corruption in the world caused by evil desires.

(2 Peter 1:3–4)

Everything men need for life and godliness is also available to women. If men may "participate in the divine nature," so may women. If men may escape the corruption of the world, so may women. How refreshing this is compared to Christensen's conclusion that "most important of all, a woman is also subject to spiritual attack," and must rely on her husband to be a "shield and protector" to his wife against the "unseen world of 'principalities and powers' (Ephesians 6:10)" (36). *Nothing* in this entire passage would suggest that the rules are any different for women than for men. Blum concurs: "Thus, in coming to know God through Christ, the believer escapes the corruption of sin; and Christ renews and restores the image of God in him" (268). Rebecca Groothuis sums it up well: "If Jesus Christ is a female believer's Lord and Savior in the same way that he is a male believer's, then surely no Christian woman has need of a man to stand in the place of Christ for her" (Pierce and Groothuis 2004, 313).

THESIS # 93

The attributes Peter urges believers to add to their faith would qualify anyone for full-time, ordained ministry.

For this very reason, make every effort to add to your faith goodness; and to goodness, knowledge; and to knowledge, self-control; and to self-control, perseverance; and to perseverance, godliness; and to godliness, brotherly kindness; and to brotherly kindness, love.

(2 Peter 1:5–7)

I have difficulty understanding why any female candidate for any ministry—whose faith in Christ is amply enhanced with goodness, knowledge, self-control, perseverance, godliness, brotherly kindness and love—is not just as qualified as any man for similar ministries.

Pastors and church leaders, please try to put yourselves in the shoes of some deeply spiritual, fully committed woman in your congregation who has consistently made *every possible effort* to exemplify the above qualifications. In fact, let's suppose that, in all honestly, her administrative gifting, commitment to Christ and ability to teach is head and shoulders above all the men in your church—maybe even yourself (I've seen it happen). Try to imagine how she feels when, time and time again, she is told that she cannot teach a mixed adult class, or preach a sermon, or serve as an elder simply because she was born *female*—even though she knows that many far less qualified and committed males continue to be elected or appointed to these same positions forever unattainable for her.

THESIS # 94

The qualities that determine effectiveness and productivity in ordained ministry are attainable and to be sought after by men and women.

For if you possess these qualities in increasing measure, they will keep you from being ineffective and unproductive in your knowledge of our Lord Jesus Christ. But if anyone does not have them, he is nearsighted and blind, and has forgotten that he has been cleansed from his past sins.

Therefore, my brothers, be all the more eager to make your calling and election sure. For if you do these things, you will never fall.

(2 Peter 1:8–10)

Those of us who have been called, commissioned or ordained to ministry would do well to regularly test ourselves against these verses. Has our growth become stagnant since our initial "call," or are we purposely advancing in the above virtues? If we are not, what gives us the right to keep holding our positions or titles? Conversely, if some women are actively maintaining these virtues, what gives anyone the right to withhold equal titles from them?

THESIS # 95

The book of Revelation frequently assumes gender-equal priesthood as every believer's right through Christ.

To him who loves us and has freed us from our sins by his blood, and has made us to be a kingdom and priests to serve his God and Father— to him be glory and power for ever and ever! Amen.

(Revelation 1:5b-6)

The above verses are similar to those later on in 5:9–10, 20:6 and 22:14. In all four cases, John explains that all believers in Christ become priests to serve our God and Father. In 5:9 we read that Christ's blood has purchased *men* for God from every tribe and "made them to be a kingdom of priests." Some have interpreted this to mean that only men will ever serve as priests, and that it will only happen in heaven. Once again, the TNIV makes it clearer by using the generic "*members* of every tribe." In addition, 1:5–6 seems abundantly clear that whatever Christ has done he has already done (past tense) for both men and women: he *has freed* us from our sins and *has made* us a kingdom of priests. These verses, coupled with 1 Peter 2:9

(you *are* a royal priesthood) leave no doubt that whatever restoration Christ has accomplished for men—for now or in eternity—he has also accomplished for women. He already calls them priests; how dare we do less?

One of the final verses of Revelation seems fitting for the close of this book: "Blessed are those who wash their robes, that they may have the right to the tree of life and may go through the gates into the city" (22:14). The first sin Adam and Eve committed was to partake of the *tree of life*—the very tree from which God commanded them not to eat. The resulting consequence was that they were both banned from the Garden of Eden (ironically, Genesis 3:22–23 only lists Adam as being banned). From the moment they were evicted from the garden until the return of the glorified Christ to heaven as the "great priest over the house of God" (Hebrews 10:21), no man or woman on earth could possibly receive the tiniest speck of grace and forgiveness from such an unapproachable God. However, when Christ sat down on his throne, he "made perfect forever those [men and women] who are being made holy" (Hebrews 10:14). Since then, our boards and ordaining councils have rightly appointed men (who, notice, are also still in the process of being made holy) to unlimited offices in the church. At the same time, many of those same boards and councils have argued that a woman's ministry must be restricted here on earth, even though her eternal salvation and rewards are just as assured as a man's. The Kroegers have said it well: "There is a serious theological contradiction in telling a woman that when she comes to faith in Christ, her personal sins are forgiven but she must continue to be punished for the sin of Eve" (22).

Conclusion

We come to the end of this brief biblical study in relation to gender equality. Some readers will still disagree with me. Others might begin to question some of their long-held beliefs, or at least be more tolerant to people they disagree with. Still others will have received clear biblical affirmation for what they had intuitively thought to be right.

In 1891, Rev. B. T. Roberts, founder of the Free Methodist Church, published *Ordaining Women: Biblical and Historical Insights*—just a year after narrowly losing the debate over women's ordination in that denomination. His poignant advice to the church he loved remains just as appropriate to many denominations today.

> We must either go back or we must go ahead. We must give her equal rights with men or we must reduce her to the servitude of by-gone ages....The present position of the churches is not only wrong but inconsistent. They concede to women too much, if Paul's words restricting her are taken literally; they concede too little if these words are to be so understood as to harmonize with the rest of the Bible....If woman, in using her voice, in praising God, or declaring His truth, in your churches, is a transgressor, then silence her at whatever cost; if she is doing right then remove all shackles and give her the liberty of the Gospel (67-68).

Eighty-three years later, at the 1974 General Conference of the Free Methodist Church, full equality was finally granted to women.

The hours of study and soul-searching required to write this little book have firmly convinced me that ministry of every type should be as fully available to qualified women as to qualified men. Three decades of professional counseling have convinced me that the happiest marriages and families are those where wives and husbands are always unconditionally, reciprocally loved as equals. For me, it all comes down to this:

From the moment the ascended Lord God, the Christ, forever co-eternal and co-equal with the Father, assumed his throne, the slightest attempt to bar even one of God's children from any ministry the Spirit assigns is to imply that the Redeemer's redemption is somehow insufficient.

~Austin Stouffer

References

Andelin, Helen. *Fascinating Womanhood*. New York: Bantam Books, 1963.

Bainton, Roland H. *Here I Stand: A Life of Martin Luther*. New York: Mentor Books, 1950.

Belleville, Linda. "Teaching and Usurping Authority." In Pierce and Groothuis, *Discovering Biblical Equality*. Downers Grove: InterVarsity Press, 2004.

Bilezikian, Gilbert. *Beyond Sex Roles*. Grand Rapids: Baker, 1985.

Blum, Edwin A. "Commentary on I & II Peter." *Expositor's Bible Commentary*. vol. 12. Grand Rapids: Zondervan, 1981.

Boomsma, Clarence. *Male and Female, One in Christ*. Grand Rapids: Baker, 1993.

Bristow, John T. *What Paul Really Said about Women*. San Francisco: HarperCollins, 1988.

Chittister, Joan D. *Heart of Flesh: A Feminist Spirituality for Women and Men*. Grand Rapids: Eerdmans, 1998.

Chrysostom, J. Quoted in John T. Bristow's *What Paul Really Said about Women*. San Francisco: Harper Collins, 1988.

Christensen, Larry. *The Christian Family*. Minneapolis: Bethany Fellowship, 1970.

Clouse, Bonnidel and Robert G. Clouse. *Women in Ministry: Four Views*. Downers Grove: InterVarsity Press, 1989.

Culver, Robert. "Let Your Women Keep Silence." Bonnidell and Robert Clouse eds. *Women in Ministry: Four Views*. Downers Grove: InterVarsity Press, 1989.

Dillow, James. *Solomon on Sex*. New York: Thomas Nelson, 1997.

Earl, Ralph. "Commentary on 1 Timothy." *Expositor's Bible Commentary*. vol. 11. Grand Rapids: Zondervan, 1981.

Fee, Gordon D. "The Priority of Spirit Gifting for Church Ministry." Pierce and Groothuis, ed. *Discovering Biblical Equality*. Downers Grove: InterVarsity Press, 2004.

Fleming, Joy Elasky. "Man and Woman in Biblical Equality." Abstracted from Doctoral Dissertation "A Rhetorical Analysis of Genesis 2–3 With Implications for A Theology of Man and Woman." University of Strasbourg, France, 1987.

Foh, Susan T. "A Male Leadership Response." Bonnidell and Robert Clouse eds. *Women in Ministry: Four Views*. Downers Grove: InterVarsity Press, 1989.

Fox, George. Quoted in O'Faolan and Martines ed. *Not in God's Image*. New York: Harper & Row, 1973.

Giles, Kevin. *The Trinity and Subordinationism*. Downers Grove: InterVarsity Press, 2002

Gilliland, B., R. James and J. Bowman. *Theories and Strategies in Counseling and Psychotherapy*. Englewood Cliffs, NJ: Prentice Hall, 1989.

Grady, J. Lee. *Ten Lies the Church Tells Women*. Lake Mary, FA: Charisma House, 2000.

Gratian, Franciscus. Quoted in O'Faolan and Martines ed. *Not in God's Image*. New York: Harper & Row, 1973.

Grenz, Stanley J. *Women in the Church: A Biblical Theology of Women in Ministry*. Downers Grove: InterVarsity Press, 1995.

————"Biblical Priesthood and Women in Ministry." Pierce and Groothuis, ed. *Discovering Biblical Equality*. Downers Grove: InterVarsity Press, 2004.

Groothuis, Rebecca Merrill. "Equal in Being, Unequal in Role." In Pierce and Groothuis, ed. *Discovering Biblical Equality*. Downers Grove: InterVarsity Press, 2004.

Grudem, Wayne and John Piper. *Recovering Biblical Manhood and Womanhood.* Wheaton: Crossway Books, 1991.

Gundry, Patricia. "Why We're Here." *Women, Authority and the Bible.* Alvera Mickelsen, ed. Downers Grove: InterVarsity Press, 1986.

————*Neither Slave nor Free.* San Francisco: Harper and Row, 1987.

————*Woman Be Free.* Grand Rapids: Zondervan, 1997.

Henry, Matthew. *Complete Commentary on the Whole Bible.* Retrieved February 8, 2007 from www.studylight.org_ 2001.

Hess, Richard. "Equal With and Without Innocence." Pierce and Groothuis, ed. *Discovering Biblical Equality.* Downers Grove: InterVarsity Press, 2004.

Howard, Carol Castor. Quoted in Bilezikian, G. *Beyond Sex Roles.* Grand Rapids: Baker, 1985.

Hull, Gretchen Gaebelein. *Equal to Serve.* Tarrytown, NY: Fleming H. Revell, 1987.

Hurley, James B. *Man and Woman in Biblical Perspective.* Grand Rapids: Zondervan, 1981.

Jewett, Paul K. *Man as Male and Female.* Grand Rapids: Eerdmans, 1975.

————*The Ordination of Women.* Grand Rapids: Eerdmans, 1980.

Johnson, Alan F. "Commentary on Revelation." *Expositor's Bible Commentary.* Vol. 12. Grand Rapids: Zondervan, 1981.

————"A Meta-Study of the Debate over the Meaning of 'Head' (Kephale) in Paul's Writings." *Priscilla Papers.* Autumn, 2006.

Johnson, Gregg T. "The Biological Basis for Gender-Specific Behavior." *Recovering Biblical Manhood and Womanhood.* John Piper and W. Grudem, ed., Wheaton: Crossway Books, 1991.

Keener, Craig S. *Paul, Women and Wives.* Peabody, MS: Hendrickson Publishers, 1992.

Kelly, J. N. D. The Pastoral Epistles." *Black's New Testament Commentaries.* London: Adam & Charles Black, 1972.

Knowles, Charles O. *Let Her Be.* Columbia, MO: KnowWell Publishing, 2005.

Kroeger, Richard Clark & Catherine Clark Kroeger. *I Suffer Not a Woman.* Grand Rapids: Baker Book House, 1992.

Liefeld, Walter L. "Your Sons and Your Daughters Shall Prophesy." *Women in Ministry: Four Views.* Downers Grove: InterVarsity Press, 1989.

Marshall, I. Howard. "Mutual Love and Submission in Marriage." *Discovering Biblical Equality.* Pierce& Groothuis, ed. Downers Grove: InterVarsity Press, 2004.

Mickelsen, Alvera, ed. *Women, Authority and the Bible.* Downers Grove: InterVarsity Press, 1986.

Morgan, Marabel. *The Total Woman.* Old Tappan, NJ: Fleming H. Revell, 1973.

O'Faolain, J. and L. Martines, ed. *Not in God's Image.* New York: Harper & Row, 1973.

Ortlund, Raymond C. "Male-Female Equality and Male Headship." *Recovering Biblical Manhood and Womanhood.* Piper & Grudem, ed. Wheaton: Crossway, 1999.

Pawson, J. David. *Leadership is Male.* E. Sussex, England: Highland Books, 1988.

Phelan, John E. Jr. *All God's People.* Chicago: Covenant Publications, 2005.

Pierce, Ronald W. & Rebecca M. Groothuis, ed. *Discovering Biblical Equality.* Downers Grove: InterVarsity Press, 2004.

Piper, John & Wayne Grudem, ed. *Recovering Biblical Manhood and Womanhood*. Wheaton: Crossway Books, 1991.

Reasoner, Mark. "Chapter 16 in Paul's Letter to the Romans: Dispensable Tagalong or Valuable Envelope?" *Priscilla Papers*. Autumn, 2006.

Roberts, Benjamin T. *Ordaining Women*. Rochester, NY: Earnest Christian Publishing House, 1891.

Rose, Sheldon D. *Working With Adults in Groups*. San Francisco: Jossey-Bass, 1990.

Schreiner, Thomas R. "The Valuable Ministries of Women in the Context of Male Leadership." *Recovering Biblical Manhood and Womanhood*. Piper and Grudem, ed. Wheaton: Crossway, 1991.

Simon, Edith. *Luther Alive*. New York: Doubleday, 1968.

Sullivan, Harry Stack. *Conceptions of Modern Psychiatry*. New York: W.W. Norton & Co., 1953.

Thiessen, Arden. *The Biblical Case for Equality*. Belleville, ON: Guardian Books, 2002.

Wood, A. Skevkngton. "Commentary on Ephesians." *Expositor's Bible Commentary*. vol. 11. Frank E. Gaebelein, ed. Grand Rapids: Zondervan, 1978.

APPENDIX I

THE REV. MRS.–Satan's Greatest Fear

This article first appeared in the Fall 1994 edition of *Priscilla Papers*, the Journal of Christians for Biblical Equality, under the ominous title, "Diabolic Directives on the Impending Feminine Advance"—a humorous, somewhat sarcastic take-off on C. S. Lewis' style of writing that many of us came to love in books such as *Screwtape Letters*.[1] Obviously, none of us knows how Satan would actually address his diabolic deputies, but Lewis' cumbersome, archaic style seems to add a certain mystique that would be lost in contemporary English. This is not the way I usually write, nor is it the way today's readers usually talk; neither does it reflect Lewis' opinion on women's place in church or home. Still, the style worked for him, so…

Over the years, I have re-read this piece a few times but (sadly) continue to think that it is still an accurate commentary on many segments of contemporary Christian society. What follows is a slight revision of the original article, prefaced by a more straightforward title. If you have already read my book, *Ninety Five More for the Door*, the article will take on greater meaning. If some of it makes no sense to you, the endnotes might help. Either way, I hope you will catch the important truths I'm trying to make, while at the same time taking it all with a grain of salt.

Austin H. Stouffer

135

THE REV. MRS.—Satan's Greatest Fear

My Dear Cohorts:

The urgency of the occasion dictates the unprecedented action on my part of corresponding personally with all of you. Suffice it to say, I would not interrupt your fiendish schedules were the matter not of utmost importance. Oh, I know that all of you have admired my optimism through the centuries concerning our eventual overthrow of the Righteous. Indeed, as one reviews the rampant lapse in moral fiber throughout the world in just the last generation of earthlings, we all have cause for gleeful gloating! Nevertheless, I am deeply distressed with a new tactic the Enemy seems to be employing.

I observe a cloud imperceptibly gathering which, when full-formed, may well pour out irreparable havoc on our devilish schemes. I speak of none other than the rapid escalation of the female gender into significant positions of authority in the Enemy's Army.

With alarming rapidity, troop after troop of His finest are defying millennia of traditions and entrenched truths by permitting women to become what they call "elders"—even commissioning them to the rank of "Reverend"—that centuries-old bastion of maleness!

Listen and tremble! If full and equal membership in the Enemy's Army will ever be offered to women, in no time His detestable band of female faithfuls could double or even triple His force of committed, qualified teachers, elders and pastors. One has visions of a "revival" for their side of proportions too staggering to contemplate. Denizens of the Deep, I am sounding the alarm for us to take up arms with deadly zeal in order to speedily repel this potentially impenetrable force.

For some of you, the memory of my masterful work in Eden has grown faint. Pity…it was indeed my finest hour! Let me recapitulate the highlights. My decision to deceive only the woman was brilliant. I can still see her standing there—disgustingly innocent, naïve, pristine. Seeing such absence of malice reminded me why I so disliked her Maker; yet, carefully garbed as I was in the beautiful body of one of His nicer creations (serpents were so magnificent then), her unsuspecting and unsullied mind became a sure target for deception. Don't misunderstand me; a talent lesser than mine might easily have failed, for she asked thoughtful, intelligent questions. But you may recall that the Enemy's command to abstain from that most desirous of trees came to Eve not from her *Maker*, but from her *mate*. Frankly, I've always relished that as a weakness in His plan—not to have roundly briefed them both as to that fearful foliage. Hence, my choice of Eve to deceive. Her knowledge of the facts seemed sparse, not having heard them gravely uttered by her Creator, but perhaps only casually mentioned by her companion. One sometimes wonders whether the male gender's ongoing inability to communicate is a created condition...

My worthies, do you see the significance of my masterful act? Oh, I could have approached them together, and *obviously* he would have yielded to *me*. He yielded to *her*, didn't he? How could he have possibly withstood the master deceiver?[2] But, you see, had they both identically shared this diabolic deed, neither could have blamed the other. Oh, what a stroke of genius! From then on, this selfish sinner would condemn his other half for causing him to sin, without any intervention on my part. Now the stage was set for the physically stronger half to forever remind his physically weaker equal that she had caused his downfall. So, together, they have become ours. Robbed of innocence, pure love and the Enemy's impeccable attributes, they are easily filled with craftiness, deception and greed.

What a glorious era it was, wherein the beast-half forced the beauty-half to be his slave. It now fell to me merely to prey on the man's vanity and perpetuate the myth that the woman was—and women are—to blame. The Jewish Talmud, early philosophers, other world religions and even pagan writers shouted the same lie: Women are inherently defective, less than the Enemy's image, somewhere below kine and slightly above swine; never let them instruct again, for they did once and ruined all.[3]

Admittedly, there were some fearful decades centuries later, during that hideous thirty-three year visitation of Enemy Number Two (or are they actually both Number One?). Had He stayed here much longer, pleasantly accepting prostitutes as equal to royalty, our cause might have fully unraveled. It annoys me to remember how He used women so prominently to observe and announce His return to them after His wretched weekend visit to our realm. Frankly, His obvious penchant to gender equality has cost us dearly. Fortunately for our side, the paternal religious structure to which He came required an all-male team of apostles—a fact we must continue to market mercilessly.

Then there was that dangerous Jew from Tarsus, whose prolific contribution to the Enemy's Manual has done us as much or more damage than the Enemy's Son. How dare he suggest that women are equal to men both in marriage and in the church! Imagine—to defy all we had labored to accomplish for thousands of years in one fell swoop, thereby declaring Jew and Gentile, slave and free, male and female all *equal!* To think of inviting women to sit in the assembly, pray and prophesy, and even to command that they be taught![4] To redefine "headship," wrenching from its age-old meaning all hint of domination and oppression, and to expect men to *love* and *serve*—yes, even to *die* for—the very one who caused their condemnation!

I slept little those nights, imagining centuries of male dominance slipping away and the ushering in of some putrid form of mushy, equal, *agape* love among the Enemy's troops, not unlike what He had originally intended. One small comfort remained: All of "fallen" humanity dies after three score years or so, and that persistent Saul/Paul fellow passed on none too soon, leaving us merely with his often ambiguous writings. Had he lived, I have no doubt he would have fleshed out his ridiculous ideologies and brought about full-scale equality between the Rev. *Mr.* and the Rev. *Mrs.* But once free of his inimitable personality, the work of his pen was easier to quell. I merely encouraged learned men (philosophers, theologians, early church fathers) to sufficiently pepper their writings with hierarchical interpretations of questionable passages, adding their own quotable castigation of women. Fully persuaded that the Manual agreed with them, they unwittingly advanced our cause. Then Augustine, Luther, Calvin and scores of others aided us immeasurably by perpetuating a doctrine so naturally palatable to men.

You may recall that many such slanted statements worked equally well for slavery—another delightful man-made institution which has served our cause well until recently. But who would have thought that the Other Side would have won that round through the efforts of a British politician, a converted slave trader and a lanky black-bearded American President, even in the face of relentless opposition from the Enemy's own troops. As with the gender issue, many of His most committed had convinced themselves of the "Divine Order of Slavery" or some such thing. I recall one of their most respected clergy vociferously arguing that overthrowing slavery would be an "assault of mistaken philanthropy, in union with infidelity, fanaticism and political expediency."[5] But the public tide of emancipation surged forward, causing His officers to reevaluate their theological moorings and find them sorely wanting. The result: a social reinterpretation of the Manual.

Hence, my dire concern today. Through no thanks to His troops, *society* has decided that it will no longer tolerate inequality shown to any group, including women. The time is upon us when all Old Boys' Clubs—societal or religious—will be brought to their knees or be tagged "chauvinistic bigots." Again, they will blushingly rewrite the interpretations of their Manual. And, ironically, as with slavery, the rewrite will be right. Lords of Iniquity, our future has never been more perilous! Women *must* not be commissioned into His Army. Oh, emancipation of slaves has not significantly increased the Enemy's fighting force—on the contrary, many of those downtrodden beings foolishly clung closer to their "Redeemer" in past affliction than in present affluence. But a world-wide force of fully commissioned, educated, Spirit-filled women may easily spell ultimate doom to our glorious forces of evil.

Enough preamble. Read carefully now as I personally instruct each of you in how to keep the Enemy's followers true to their man-made traditions while still blind to the truth. Here are several tried and true tactics that will require your full proficiency if we are ever to maintain dominance over this planet. First and foremost, we must keep emphasizing what traditional theologians call the "Created Order." At all cost, keep them convinced that Adam's direct creation from dust shows ownership and superiority over Eve, who merely came from Adam's rib. Impress on them the logic of that thought: woman is merely an *appendage* to serve man. This creation-order teaching can be neatly augmented by Paul's letter to the Corinthian followers, where he states that woman came *from* man and is *for* man. Do anything to distract them from the apostle's very next statement: "In the Lord, however, woman is not independent of man nor man independent of woman." And by all means, don't let it cross their minds that the Enemy (too generously, I think) gave both genders an equal mandate to rule this planet before they chose my rule.[6]

A close cousin to the Created Order fallacy, and one of equal success up to now, revolves around the matter of authority. The longer we can perpetuate the Old Boys' Club mentality the better—it has worked in service clubs for years. Keep them convinced that all of their officers (elders, presbyters, clergy) *must* be male. It helps to remind them that virtually all of the significant leaders on their side have been male. Frankly, authority is such an easy doctrine to expound, for it quite naturally caters to male pride. As "head of his house," each little Napoleon stands in daily danger of wanting more and more power until he is like his Maker (a concept that has obsessed me for centuries).

As pride flourishes, men will redefine legitimate male uniqueness as superiority, consequently reducing female attributes to an inferior status. Oh yes, there is great advantage in accentuating gender differences. Encourage men's rugged, bossy, *macho* cravings in everything from adult videos to monster trucks to moose hunting to combat rifles, to climbing corporate ladders. That's what real men do. Conversely, ensure that such things as tears, empathy, compassion, intuition and relationships continue to be the sole domain—even attractiveness of—the weaker sex. With minimal coaching and continued distortion of their Manual's teaching, both will stay convinced that coolness, objectivity and brute force are essential for leadership, and must, therefore, only be performed by men. If all goes well, the fools will never see the abundance of so-called feminine qualities in the Enemy's Son. Oh, how it galls me to recall how tender and compassionate He could be!

Indeed, among Christian men these days there is a growing trend toward relationships, "twelve step" programs and the like. How embarrassing to see males being vulnerable and accountable, admitting their dysfunction in front of an entire group! Some of them are actually staying home and *enjoying* an evening with their own children while Mother is out on the town. This blurring of established roles can only damage our carefully honed image of the aloof, authoritarian husband-father who merely condescends to baby-sit on occasion. Our world is in deep trouble.

Now, let me raise a further delightful twist to male leadership. With very little coaxing on our part, any sincere young husband desirous of being a firm but loving "head" of his home can easily be made to act less like them and more like us. All it takes is a teething baby, a sexually unyielding wife, a layoff at the office or a fight with the in-laws, and those attributes which put him in charge will make him a monster. Psychological or physical abuse of wife or children may speedily follow as his power becomes corrupted. Similarly, a wife who initially chooses to joyfully submit can be dragged through enough bumps of marriage that she views herself as a helpless slave. Whether she then divorces him or stoically accepts her fate, our cause has once again been advanced.

Such teaching over the years has developed an interesting side effect. Women have come to believe that they have no mechanical prowess or objectivity, but must rely on their men in these areas. Hence, they have fallen upon manipulation to get their way, undermining male authority with the promise of demurely meeting every male desire from office to kitchen to bedroom. Thus, the "head" remains convinced God has endowed him to lead while his cold objectivity lacks the intuition to see that the neck is forever turning the head!

Another amusing, though effective, way to accentuate male superiority is through the Annual General Conferences, Synods or General Assemblies of churches, to which delegates are commissioned to attend. Schedule some workshops only for men and others only for women. Then, ensure that one long hot day of each conference be dedicated to "Ladies' Society" meetings wherein the fairer sex don their finery and elect each other to committees of no consequence to our cause—just be sure that everyone gets either a position or a plaque for some reason. For weeks ahead, create an aura of mystery about the guest speaker (a woman), but be sure her topic turns out to be as harmless as "Embroidering Communion Tablecloths" or "Making Yourself Attractive to your Man." Meanwhile, "their men" will receive solid spiritual food from a renowned, imported exegete (an ordained and lettered man). Now and then one of the stronger weaker vessels may momentarily wish to sample the male fare, but propriety and tradition will ultimately keep her in her place. Hence, both will return from the conference with exuberant reports of how they were singularly blessed.

Oh yes—I almost omitted one of the greatest weapons in your arsenal: Original Language Debates. Take, for instance, that delightfully simple Greek word, *kephale*. Oh, the satisfaction it has brought me to see His best scholars waste months, years, lifetimes in relentless documentation of usages of that word to support their cause. Their obsession to know what "man as head" means has kept both genders from letting the Enemy's Son be *their* head! Exquisite joy! Keep them bickering over such minutiae as whether or not prophecy is inferior to preaching, what the "early traditions" really are, can the extant manuscripts be trusted—oh yes, and the head-covering and "because of the angels" passage. How delightful to watch earthlings embrace us at an unprecedented rate while their best "authoritative preachers" use all their energy to defend their male turf! It reminds me of the Most Venerable Screwtape's sage advice to Wormwood some years ago: "Leave *them* to discuss whether 'Love,' or patriotism, or celibacy, or candles on altars, or teetotalism, or education, are 'good' or 'bad.' Can't you see, there's no answer."[7]

Of great consternation to me these days is the unexpected increase of women in seminaries—those pesky institutions which serve as boot camp apprenticeships for the Enemy's full-time Army. True, we have successfully disarmed the firepower of most of these schools, so that they are little more than a religious presence with such diluted curricula that their graduates, male or female, pose no real threat to us. But these days, even the so-called "*evangelical*" seminaries are accepting women—keen, intelligent, committed students bent on dragging earthlings out of our darkness into His despicable light. Our strongest hope is to fall back on the "authoritative preaching" tactic. By all means, let women be employed as teachers of children and other women, leaders of day care centers or as "parish workers," but never let them do authoritative teaching from a pulpit! Most of them still harbor vestiges of guilt about even being in the full-time Army, so will never aspire to the higher ranks reserved for males. You will notice much similarity between this and how we have abused missionary women for decades.

For those churches progressive enough to hire a female pulpit pastor, it would be wise to steer a certain type their way. I'm thinking of the striking, well-dressed dramatic candidate who knows how to coordinate style and color to accentuate her attributes. Better yet if she be a shallow thinker, one who will use the pulpit to spin doctrinally true but harmless homilies with just the right amount of wholesome innocence and seeming flirtatiousness. In no time, wives will hate her, men will lust after her, traditional leadership will say, "I told you so," and the era of authoritative female preaching in that church will abruptly end!

Less attractive women, or those few who blend beauty and modesty with discretion, are of much greater concern, especially if they are also deeply spiritual and forceful exegetes of His Manual (and many are!). Here, you must unearth and magnify some tangential malady: a lisp, perhaps, or a physical deformity, or some annoying habit of throat-clearing, or—my preference—have her young child keep toddling up to the pulpit with either pitiful whinings or temper tantrums. Whereas the congregants have dutifully endured years of tepid ramblings from the previous male shepherd under the now-tattered rubric, "Thou shalt not touch the Lord's anointed!" the slightest blemish in the shepherdess will soon have her searching for other sheepfolds. Likely as not, those sheepfolds will be less evangelical. It falls to our benefit that many of these gifted, brilliant women finally despair of the undue criticisms railed against them from traditional conservatives. Yet, convinced that they can, want to and feel called to lead and preach, they may rein in their theological tenets and brokenly seek the employ of some waffling liturgical group, New Age gathering or cult. It matters not; once again, we score!

My epistle grows too lengthy. Comrades, I trust I have inspired you to new levels of service. Try not to yield to depression as you contemplate the worst of scenarios. Should the Enemy's side ever attempt to initiate gender equality, there may yet be a heretofore unmentioned blessing for us. Remember that these same bright, gifted women are yet dual-natured creatures of what they call "the Fall." We can only hope that the headiness of equality may stir in them a lust for retributive dominance over those who have so long

145

oppressed them. Who knows but that we may well enjoy centuries of *female* authority! Swings of the pendulum are common among earthlings, both in political and religious arenas. Yet one day, the inevitable will surely happen. You, too, should shudder to think of the accuracy of that wretched Manual and its Author. His sons *and daughters* will prophesy before that final holocaust.

Leave me now to reflect on my past triumph of wounding that most perfect of heels. The clouds gather; ultimately we shall suffer the inevitable crush of her offspring…[8]

In the meantime, I remain:

Your Affectionate Father Below

Endnotes to Appendix I

1. C.S. Lewis, *Screwtape Letters*. (New York: MacMillan, 1961)

2. Here the writer may be suggesting a possible interpretation of 1 Timothy 2:14 (Adam was not deceived; it was the woman who was deceived…) as meaning that the Deceiver chose to tempt Eve, perhaps because her "lesser knowledge" made her an easier target. On the other hand, Adam still chose to sin, even though he was directly commanded by God not to do so, and he did not have to personally face the Deceiver as Eve did. This may suggest an even greater culpability on Adam's part (1 Corinthians 15:22).

3. Leading church father St. John Chrysostom (345–407 AD) is quoted as saying, "The woman taught once and ruined all. On this account…let her not teach…The whole female race transgressed." From "Works of Chrysostom: Homilies on Timothy" in *Select Library of Nicene Fathers*. This and many other remarkable quotations have been collected by J. O'Faolain and L. Martines in *Not in God's Image* (NewYork: Harper and Row, 1973).

4. The author's suggestion that Paul commands women to teach finds its basis in 1 Timothy 2:11, usually translated, "A woman should learn in quietness and full submission." The Greek *manthaneto* ('should learn') is present active imperative, and could legitimately be translated, "I command that women be taught (or learn)." The same applies to v. 12 ("I do not permit a woman to teach" may mean, "I am *presently* not permitting women to teach"—that is, until they have been taught.

5. Over 100 years ago, the Rev. B. T. Roberts wrote a delightful little book called *Ordaining Women* (Rochester, NY: Earnest Christian Publishing House, 1891), in which he quotes the Right Rev. John Henry Hopkins, Episcopal Bishop of the diocese of Vermont, attempting to prove that human slavery was supported by "the authority of the Bible, the writings of the Fathers, the decrees of councils, the concurrent judgment of Protestant divines, and the [USA] Constitution." He characterizes any efforts to overthrow slavery as the "assaults of mistaken philanthropy, in union with infidelity, fanaticism, and political expediency" (p. 12). One can only ponder how much of the traditionalists' platform today is still fueled by similar factors.

6. It seems more than accidental that the mandate to rule all things (Genesis 1:26–28) was given *jointly* to both Adam and Eve.

7. C. S. Lewis, p. 98.

8. A subtle reference to the prophetic properties of Genesis 3:15.

APPENDIX II

How to Use this Book as a Bible Study or Sunday School Guide

Because this book is specifically written for lay people, Bible study leaders and Sunday school teachers may find its content helpful as a study guide. Of course, your group may approach it any way you or they wish; however, the two tables below may give your leader some guidelines as to how to "walk through" the book in one or two quarters of 12 studies each.

Outline for 24 studies (six months or two quarters):

Study #	Thesis	Study #	Thesis
1	1–4	13	35–37
2	5–8	14	38–40
3	9–13	15	41–45
4	14	16	46–51
5	15–16	17	52–57
6	17–19	18	58–63
7	20–21	19	64–69
8	22–23	20	70–73
9	24–25	21	74–78
10	26–28	22	79–81
11	29–32	23	82–88
12	33–34	24	89–95

Outline for 12 studies (three months or one quarter):

Study #	Thesis	Content	Study #	Thesis	Content
1	1–6	Genesis 1–2	7	41–45	II Corinthians
2	7–13	Genesis 3	8	46–51	Galatians
3	14–16	Proverbs, Song of Songs	9	52–63	Ephesians
4	17–22	Matthew, Mark, John	10	64–72	Philippians, Colossians
5	23–28	Acts, Romans	11	73–84	I & II Timothy
6	29–40	I Corinthians	12	85–95	Titus, Revelation

PLEASE NOTE: This twelve week study is structured so that each week the class will be looking at a different book (or books) of the Bible. Because of the volume of material, you may wish to ask different members of your group to pre-read one or more thesis, then come prepared to lead that part of the study.

Men's Study:

If you're interested in helping men become more sensitive and relational to their spouse and family, consider starting a weekly men's study based on this book—or just discuss certain thesis statements that might be most helpful. Perhaps they've only heard the "head of the house" arguments, and never thought about how life-changing (and marriage changing!) it becomes when a husband genuinely manifests a humble, self-sacrificing, Christ-like love for his wife and children.

Women's Study:

If your church is average, it is fairly safe to assume that some women struggle with the well-intentioned but domineering—even abusive—attitude of their husbands, fathers or employers. Although too shy to speak up in a mixed group, they may benefit from a careful study of these same passages and how, when properly understood and applied, their love for and relationship with their husbands can dramatically improve.

Inter-church Studies:

Many churches are too small to launch their own study on this topic. Why not consider inviting other churches of the same or similar denomination to join you one night a week for a twelve-week study or Saturday morning workshop?

Additional Resources and Options:

There are literally hundreds of good books and articles available that offer the same biblical approach to these passages. Please check out the website for an organization called *Christians for Biblical Equality*, and consider taking out an individual or church membership. Their excellent quarterly publications will keep you and your church well informed on the best scholarship available, recent books published, and information on how you can organize a local chapter of CBE. You'll find this and much more at (www.cbeinternational.org).

Please Stay in Touch

Here are a few sample questions for you to ponder:

1. Do you basically agree or disagree with most of my "points"?

2. Would you be comfortable ordaining women to any and all ministry positions?

3. Which passages of Scripture remain the most difficult or controversial to you?

4. What do you think "headship" means and should look like in a home?

5. What church denomination are you affiliated with?

I would be delighted to hear your answers to questions like these, and to know what you think of my little book (even if you disagree with it all). If I can be of any assistance in your ongoing study of this topic, please e-mail me (below). All correspondence will be treated with the utmost confidence.

Austin H. Stouffer

95more@tbaytel.net

Or mail to :

A. H. Stouffer—95MORE
Site 3 Comp 31 RR 13
Thunder Bay, ON P7B 5E4
Canada

Author Index